LYNDWO
PROVINCl ⎯ᴇ

THE TEXT OF THE CANONS THEREIN
CONTAINED, REPRINTED FROM THE
TRANSLATION MADE IN 1534

EDITED BY

J. V. BULLARD AND H. CHALMER BELL

Proctors in the York Convocation.

LONDON

THE FAITH PRESS, LTD.

22 BUCKINGHAM STREET, CHARING CROSS, W.C. 2

SCHEDULE OF TITULI AND CHAPTERS

FOREWORD.

THE justification for this book is the conviction that familiarity with the ancient canons of the Church of England will do much to prepare the way for the solution of some of the problems with which we are faced.

The experiment in legislative freedom which the Church Assembly represents made inevitable some attempt to deal with the long overdue business of liturgical reform. That, for the moment, has suffered a serious set-back, but not before it had taught the lesson, that no matter how excellent the revised formularies might be, smooth working, after many years of chaos, could only be secured by means of a system of Church courts, which commanded the allegiance and respect of all Church-people.

Nor did it require much further consideration to arrive at the conclusion that, equal in importance to the courts themselves is the law which they would be called upon to administer.

Strange to say, however, this did not appear to be a prime necessity to the minds of those whose business it would be to administer the law. Obviously, what was needed was a commission, representative of all the interests involved, to work side by side with the Ecclesiastical Courts Commission, and consider the whole question of Ecclesiastical Law; to explain what was obscure; to disentangle what was involved; to earmark what was obsolete for repeal in a proper manner, and what was inadequate, for amendment; and so prepare the way for consolidation, and for the issue of a Codex, to be available for reference, not only by the ecclesiastical lawyer, but by the unprofessional student and seeker after information, especially by the clergy, who are naturally expected to know what the law is, and to keep within it.

The first step in this direction was left to private enter-prise. Eventually, the Lower House of the Convocation

of York petitioned for the appointment of a committee
to " provide an exposition of the Canon Law." The
Committee reported, but the consideration of the report
was delayed for a long time by the pressure of other
business.

As might be expected, the report revealed the fact that
there were widely divergent opinions upon certain points,
and the Committee itself came to the conclusion that a
large, weighty and representative commission was the
proper body to deal with the matter. Accordingly, the
Lower House petitioned the President of the Convocation
of York to take the necessary steps for the appointment
of such a commission.

That is the position at present. The editors of this
volume, who were members of the York Committee, are
strongly of opinion that the whole subject suffers from
having been invested with an esoteric character. They
decided, therefore, to prepare an English text of the
Canons collected by William Lyndwood in the early
fifteenth century, in the commentary which he called the
Provinciale, which received the imprimatur of the Convocations both of Canterbury and York.

A translation of the text of these Canons was in exist-
ence. This translation was made in 1534, and it is evident
from the preface to it, that it was undertaken at the
instance of King Henry VIII.

The text here printed is that of this sixteenth century
translator. The chapter divisions and headings have been
added to correspond with the Latin text of the
Provinciale, published at Oxford in 1676. Only such
notes have been added as are necessary to make clear
obscurities in the text. The Latin of the enacting word
in each canon has been inserted in brackets in order to
indicate the stringency of the different canons.

Familiarity on the part of the clergy and others with
the written law of the English Church, as practised at the
beginning of the Reformation, will, we hope, materially
assist in the work of consolidation and revision.

To anyone who has read the report of the Lausanne

Conference, two other questions stand out strong and
large.

I. Is it possible to reconcile the Episcopal Churches
and the Congregational Churches?

The restoration of a properly functioning synod holds
out the hope of an affirmative answer. For, with the
synod properly functioning, the Bishop's office would be
limited as originally to matters of Order, and the exercise
of discipline over priests would be with the synod of
priests (no doubt with the Bishop as their executive
officer); and the control of policy would be with the
whole Church.

II. Is it possible to construct a basis for Union between
the Churches of America and those of Europe?

Again an affirmative answer seems possible if the
American Churches accept a territorial basis of organisa-
tion.

Apart from the Lausanne Conference, all who feel the
need of readjusting the present position in England may
also find hope in the restoration of the synod.

For the study of these solutions also, some familiarity
with the Ancient Canons will be necessary. This end will
also be served by this small volume. Whatever be
Lyndwood's personal merits as a lawyer, whatever the
limitations of his *Provinciale,* for good or ill, it is as a
fact the only body of provincial Canon Law in this
country which has received the unfettered and free consent of both Convocations and has also received the full
authority of the State by an Act of Parliament.

J. V. B.
H. C. B.

INTRODUCTION.

I.—By J. V. BULLARD.

THEY were very puzzling people—these Christians—to the officials of the Roman Empire. What was to be done with them? Apart from their eccentric standards in private life were they in any sense a danger to the body politic? Were they likely to disturb the Pax Romana?

That question took time to answer. Meanwhile, the Christians themselves held their first councils (recorded in Acts of the Apostles) and laid down the barest possible fundamental principles which were to govern their society and the practical application of them to the difficulties which they had so far encountered.

Then the Roman Empire made up its mind—and made a mistake. The Christians were to be classed among the illegal societies. The " Persecutions " were the consequence. It was a mistake and was recognised as such after three hundred years of attempted suppression in Constantine's Edict of 314.

But that mistake of the Empire was the greatest possible blessing to the Church. Through ten generations of enthusiasm the Church was precluded from holding general councils, and making rules and standing orders. The churches accumulated experience instead; and, as they were widely scattered among different peoples, they accumulated variations in expression of the same truths : they accumulated variations of discipline, and of ritual to express the same worship.

Consequently, when the Church at large was recognised as a legal society in 314 and the first world-wide Council was held at Nicæa in 325, the body of Rules or Canons and the Constitutional Procedure drawn up there were not merely intelligent or tentative anticipations of what might happen in the future, but were the record of things which had occurred in the past and of the method of dealing with them which had been found efficient. They thus avoided the snag that catches most constitution mongers —the snag of legislating for imaginary contingencies.

The silence of the Church during these first three hundred years is generally misunderstood, and consequently misinterpreted into an indication that there was no " organised " religion in the Early Church before the Œcumenical Councils suddenly invented Canon Law and the Creed.

The things had been going on : but the Church had had no opportunity—through the interference of the State—to formulate her practice and her doctrine authoritatively between the Councils of Jerusalem and that of Nicæa. Unauthoritatively, of course, as we all know, it had been done by private writers from time to time and as point after point occurred, and each Church or group of Churches had acted as best it could in its own limited authority.

Although the forced inactivity in Church legislation during the first 300 years was productive of good, the arrears were considerable. It is nothing to be surprised at that it took at least four general councils and over a hundred and fifty years to bring things up to date and to lay down a scheme of constitutional practice sufficiently comprehensive to cover the general needs of the world. Some people claim six general or œcumenical, or worldwide councils as binding in all the Churches : but, so far as I know, no one refuses such authority to the first four.

Meanwhile, it is necessary to be severely logical; and to point out that even if one takes S. Vincent of Lerins' definition of what is binding upon all Churchmen, namely, what has been accepted " semper, ubique, ab omnibus," yet that definition is not exhaustive since the general Council of Nicæa (Can. 5) lays it down that Provincial Synods are to meet twice a year and that Diocesan Synods are to exercise authority. A Churchman is therefore bound to accept not only what has always been accepted everywhere by every Christian, but he is also bound to accept as valid in addition thereto the decisions of the

Synods of the Province and of the diocese to which he belongs—always provided, of course, that neither of these is contrariant to the decisions of the larger area, and superior jurisdiction within which either is included. Apart from General Councils, the Province (presided over by the Metropolitan) has generally been the largest unit of jurisdiction in the West, and the Patriarchate, or group of Provinces, has sometimes been so regarded in the East. Any appeal from them to another province was punished by suspension. (Concil: Ephesus 7 and 8[1] and Chalcedon 4—8.)

Denebert, Bishop of Salisbury, 793, in his consecration oath, accepted the first six general councils.

Hooker[2] shows that " the first four general councils are acknowledged by the law of England."

There is no doubt that they are acknowledged by the Church to-day as having authority, as well as by the Law, since in the consecration of Bishops reference is made to the ancient canons.

Starting from that basis of the canons of General Councils which are binding upon us, we next proceed to the consideration of the canons framed by our own English Provincial Councils—which are also binding upon us. What are they?

To answer the question we must patiently begin at the beginning.

The Teutonic background to the English Parish left the English parish priest in the position of his predecessor

---

[1] Lambert in *Codex Canonum Ecclesiæ Universæ*, 1868 (R. D. Dickinson) gives these as Canons. So do Zonaras Johnson and Migne. Bruns stops at Canon 6. But whether canons or transactions, the passage is the work of the Council of Ephesus. " And the very same shall be observed also in other dioceses and provinces everywhere, so that none of the Bishops most beloved by God do assume any other province that was not formerly and from the beginning, subject to him, or to his predecessors. But if any one have even assumed, and by force have reduced it under him, he must give it up lest the Canons of the Fathers be transgressed."

To lie under the sentence of the synod is defined in Canon 7 as deposition for a bishop, degradation for a priest.

[2] *Ecclesiastical Polity*, Book VIII., ch. ii. § 17.

the heathen priest. That is to say, apart from his ordination, he was practically independent of all bishops: and on the other hand he was strictly local—the priest of *a* Church, not a priest of *the* Church. He was regarded as being married to his Church. That is why, although his patron, the Lord of the Manor, was his master, yet he was unmovable and stopped at his Church until he died.[3] His stipend approximated to that of two freemen of his village and the patron made a profit out of his Church.

It was not a desirable state of affairs, and has left the mark of its heathen origin on us still in the patronising treatment of the village priest by the people at "the big house," in the "rapprochement" between the squire and the bishop as against the parson; and in the sale of advowsons.

But better things soon prevailed and the interests of the flock of Christ came to be considered as of more importance than the lord's profit or the priest's independence. On the evidence of many cartularies and especially of Textus Roffensis many laymen donated some of their manors (including churches) to Bishops or monasteries, who were expected to make a profit out of them—and did so.

The donor and his family continued also to make a profit out of his donated estate, the original donor receiv-

---

[3] Nicæa XV. and XVI. Chalcedon VI. Canons of Edgar VIII. This is Chalcedon VI.:

No one, either Priest or Deacon, or, in short, any of those in the ecclesiastical order, must be ordained at large, but he who is to be ordained must be specially assigned to a Church in city or village, martyrium or monastery. But the holy Synod has decreed that they who have been ordained at large, have received such imposition of hands to no purpose, and that they cannot anywhere officiate, to the reproach of the ordainer.

This is Nicæa XV.:

By reason of the great disorder and disturbances which exist, it seems good that the custom which is found in some places, contrary to the Canon, be wholly laid aside, so that neither bishop, priest, nor deacon remove from city to city. But if any after the decision of the holy and great Synod should attempt any such thing, or resign himself up to any such practice, all the proceedings shall be entirely null, and he shall be restored to the Church for which he was ordained bishop or presbyter.

ing a lump sum at the time of the donation, and his successors each receiving a lump sum on the occasion of confirming the donation. Such a thing as a perpetual outright donation in fee simple which would bind heirs and successors appears to have been unrecognised in this country before Dunstan secured his verdict, at Erith, from the Sheriff of the county, in this case against Leofsunu in the matter of 720 acres at Wouldham, by an appeal to " ecclesiastical law books."[4] That case marked the point where the Anglo-Teutonic system came into conflict with Ecclesiastical Law, which over-rode it.

But this process of donations brought the parish priest within the jurisdiction of the Bishop, who either replaced the Lord of the Manor as master in cases where the manor was given to the See, or else, in cases where the manor was given to the Monastery, exercised jurisdiction as visitor of the monastery according to the ecclesiastical law.[5]

At present there was no mention of the authority of Rome : which canonically was excluded by Canon 8 of Ephesus. Dunstan's ecclesiastical law books cannot have been a codex of Roman Canon Law for none such existed at that time. They might, and probably did include, the Canons of the six general councils, the Canons of Cloveshoo (747), the Canons of Chelsea (787), the Canons of Edgar (958), and those sections of Justinian which dealt with Church Property and appear to be referred to in Canon 14 of Chelsea.

The passage in Textus Roffensis makes the sheriff accept the Archbishop's oath without corroboration or further evidence. But as a matter of fact outside that technical acceptance there were furnished the oaths of 1,000 notables of the county in confirmation of the Archbishop. It was a typically English fusion of two systems ; and a particularly happy one, since agreement was estab-

---

[4] *Textus Roffensis,* cap. 73.
[5] Chalcedon, Canon IV.

lished between the ecclesiastical law books and the system of compurgation.[6]

The transition of the parish priest from the personal control of the Lord of the Manor to the control of the Bishop lasted some time and was not actually effected until the thirteenth century. In fact, some Bishops still seem to regard themselves as masters of their parish priests on the Teutonic basis, rather than as exercising constitutional jurisdiction over them through the Diocesan Synod.

That transition of Religious authority from the Anglo-Teutonic pre-Christian system to the system of Ecclesiastical Law took longer. Because, though at the beginning of the transition Rome did not come into the picture as exercising authority but only as giving advice, she yet held the attraction of possessing an almost complete system which appealed to the Bishops and the Lawyers. They were more or less ready to accept the claims to jurisdiction which Rome subsequently made because they left them autocratic rather than constitutional masters.

On the other hand, the parish priests, identified by their tithe and glebe with the yeoman stock of the country, were strenuously concerned in preserving local customs and Teutonic instincts for freedom and independence of all foreign control. Nor did they find any justification in past history or present needs for suppressing the authority of their own Provincial Synods, which expressed so well their Teuton instinct that a man is only bound by laws which he has helped to make. The synod of Chelsea, in which both Archbishops and some suffragans and priests from each Province took part, uses these words :—

"Therefore we (i.e. the Chelsea synod) *advise* that the synodical decrees of the six general Councils,

---

[6] Another similar conflict between "judicial" systems is recorded by Jocelin of Brakelond. Ketel, a free tenant of the Cellarer, was charged with theft. Because he lived outside the gate he was tried by ordeal. Vanquished in trial by battle, he was hanged. If he had lived inside the borough, he would have acquitted himself by the oaths of his neighbours.

with the decrees of the Roman Pontiffs be read with attention and that the state of the Church be reformed according to the *pattern* described therein, that no *novelty* be introduced lest there be a schism in the Church of God."[7]

It was Saint Augustine, not the Pope, who appointed the first Archbishop of York. In France, in Spain, in Africa, Metropolitans received confirmation of their election from their Provincial Synods, not from the Pope. In Italy itself the same thing was true of the Metropolitans of Ravenna and Milan.[8]

That was the past which the Anglo-Teuton priests and people knew, and they were slow to move from a position which met their needs satisfactorily and was familiar.

In that conservative attitude they were supported by the landed classes. This accounts for the fact that right through English History the Statute Book reflects the Teutonic independence of Rome and supports the authority of the Provincial Synod, while the bishops and ecclesiastical lawyers (with exceptions who were always conspicuous) lean towards Rome and autocracy, and Roman Canon Law, and lean away from synods which give expression to the influence of the parochial clergy.

Roughly speaking, lawlessness began with the Bishops.

Nevertheless, it is the fact, all through this long period of transition from the missionary stage of the English Church, in a semi-barbarous country with preponderating heathen and local survivals, to the settled stage of an established Church in a civilised country, it was necessary and natural that some *pattern* should be kept before the eyes of the statesmen who steered the Church's Course.

The only settled pattern available was the Church of Rome. That was civilised and had a long history. It was natural that, when difficulties occurred, the heads of the other churches should consult her. Just as natural as for the Bishop of Madras, or Vermont, or the Arch-

[7] Ch. iv. page 35. Gee and Hardy, *Documents.*
[8] Thomassin, *Ancienne et Nouvelle Discipline de l'Eglise,* Part II. Liv. II., chap. xix.

bishop of Capetown or of Melbourne to consult the Arch·
bishop of Canterbury in these days.

But the consultation of Rome did not originally imply
any jurisdiction of Rome, more than the parallel consultation of Canterbury would imply the jurisdiction of
Canterbury now.

Yet the modern claim to universal jurisdiction by the
Papacy seems to have grown out of such references and
consultations.

We may remember that Hilary promoted the first
National Synod, that Gelasius based precedence between
churches on synodical decrees, that Gregory the Great
repudiated the idea of an universal patriarchate as anti-
Christian; that Dunstan got the Pope's support but was
unanimously *elected* Archbishop of Canterbury *by the
Province* and subsequently refused requests from the
Pope, which he could not have done if his appointment
was due to the Pope's authority. (Thomassin.)

The Synod of Chelsea, Canon 8, (page 35, Gee and
Hardy *loc. cit.*) says "that ancient privileges conferred on
Churches by the Holy Roman See be preserved by all.
But if any have been granted contrary to the Canonical
decrees in compliance with wicked men, let them be can-
celled."

This surely disproves the view that Rome was the
paramount source of authority.

Further, Thomassin, a great Roman authority, says that
"the letters which the patriarchs exchanged with one
another and the Pope at the commencement of their
episcopate were only letters of religious civility."[9]

Similar civilities were the report of the findings by the
Synod of Chelsea through special messengers and the
report from the Pope to our Provincial Synods when
there had been some real progress made in Roman legislation, such as the Decretals.

Finally, summing up the whole matter, Thomassin[10]

[9] *Ancienne et Nouvelle Discipline de l'Eglise,* Part II. Liv. II.,
chap. xix.
[10] Part II. Liv. II., chap xxx. 1.

says that papal jurisdiction over foreign churches was a matter of growth dating from the time of Charlemagne.

If we review our Church History down to the time of the Conquest, on the principle sketched out above, and fill out each instance with all the others available, we are left in exactly Thomassin's position. At that point of time it was undoubtedly true to say that the Pope had no jurisdiction in our Church or Country, only the moral influence of the advice of an elder brother. Like other elder brothers, he was sometimes " bossy."

It is true to say that at the Norman Conquest the Provincial Canon Law was that produced by Dunstan at Erith.

Thomassin goes on to say that the slow growth of the Papal universal jurisdiction is a proof of its divine origin.

The question is, did it ever exist? The claims grew, but did the thing itself? The answer seems to be a most emphatic negative.

That brings us to the Norman Conquest.

After the Norman Conquest, the first big thing that happened in our Ecclesiastical Law was the Council of Otho, in 1236.

I want to claim the Constitutions of Otho as an English document on English authority, and to do so on the evidence of Otho in the Constitutions themselves, and of Matthew Paris, and of John Atho, who was Otho's secretary and edited the Constitutions.

The story begins in 1226, when Otho, Cardinal and Legate, came begging to England for the relief of the poor lawyers at Rome who were so often accused of charging excessive fees.

The suggestion which Otho brought from the Pope was that, as the King and the Diocesan Bishops shared the patronage of the Canonries in the Cathedrals, the King and the Bishop should each give one canonry in each Cathedral to the Pope for the benefit of the poor lawyers who had not " sufficient " to live upon.

The English ecclesiastical mind, according to the very human Paris, thoroughly enjoyed such monstrous

humility and proceeded to write rhyming couplets and
to pass them round at Otho's expense :

> " Sufficiency springs from the soul, not from the
> goods in your train :
> " Deficiency springs from the hole, not in your
> purse, but your brain."

Then, after laughing at him, they answer him with
serious faces : " This touches the Crown, we cannot deal
with it."

This is really in Matthew Paris : and it really represents the English view and practice of the Jus Patronatus.

And so Otho, a beggar of some magnificence, went to
stay in country houses until the King was pleased to
answer the request. The King's reply is given in Matthew
Paris, Vol. III. page 109, year 1226.

> " These matters of yours, in which the Lord Pope
> uses his persuasions upon us, have regard to the
> whole breadth of Christianity; and since we are, as
> it were, in the outer-most regions of the established
> world, when we shall have seen how the rest of the
> kingdoms have comported themselves towards such
> exactions, the Lord Pope will not find people readier
> in pliancy, when we shall have had an example from
> other kingdoms."

Thus Otho was turned down.

Now does that look as if Otho could come here because
he was a Cardinal and a Legate and impose the Pope's
wishes on either Church or State?

No better fate awaited Otho when, in the same year,
he made the same request, for the same reasons, at Lyons.
The assembled Bishops of the French Church turned him
down. It is not necessary to elaborate the point that the
Pope as such had very little authority over foreign
nations or their Churches.

Those who have enjoyed reading the English Statutes
of the Realm at large and other works of a less formal
but less interesting nature like Prescott, Motley, Froude,
and Lavisse, will recall numerous similar instances in

which papal claims of authority were constantly being refused.

It is true that the demand in 1226 might be regarded as a request for charity. It might even be pleaded that the authority of the Pope was not involved. But in view of what followed it did not seem fair to leave out this part of the story, as it gives the atmosphere that clung round Otho, and exhibits as an accepted dogma the desire for uniformity of action on the part of all the national churches.

The Decretum of Gratian had been published in 1150, and at once had won wide acceptance on its own merits in England, as elsewhere, as a record of useful cases to consult, though it had not then, and has never had papal authority.[11] It never was anything but a private collection. But in 1234 the Decretals obtained the official sanction of the Pope who followed rather than led the acceptance of the Codification.

Possibly, as a matter of mere civility—possibly to show the Pope that in matters which did not affect Constitutional points there was everything to be gained by an approximate uniformity of Church Law, in 1236, Henry invited Otho to come once more to England; not to beg, this time, but to help in the reform of English Canon Law.

The Canons of Edgar were now 300 years old. The invitation alone is evidence of important differences between English Canon Law and the Decretals.

The Magnates were indignant, says Paris, at the invitation.

" The King upsets everything, laws, faith, promises; in everything he transgresses. Now he marries a foreigner without advice, now secretly summons a Legate —he is always changing the whole kingdom—now he gives away his stuff and now wants it back again."

---

[11] For members of the Roman Communion, the matter is summed up in the words of Benedict XIV. (*De Syn. Diœc.* lib. VII. c. 15, n 6.) ni fallor : " tantum auctoritatis habent, quantum ex se habuissent, si nunquam in Gratiani Decreto inserta forent."

The Archbishop of Canterbury objected to the calling of the Legate knowing that " thence to the prejudice of his own dignity great boasting was hanging over the kingdom." A true prophet ! But the King had issued the invitation and Otho was coming as an invited guest, and not the emissary of the Pope. Notwithstanding which Otho wrote to all the Bishops and asked them to meet him " to hear the authentic letter of the Lord Pope about the plenary power of the legation committed to him and to deal with the reformation of the English Church and to hold a Council in his presence." That shows, of course, what Otho meant.

By his dry record Matthew Paris leaves no doubt, though he makes no comment. Otho went on to order grandiose preparations for the Council, and the Archbishops, Bishops, Abbots and Priors, etc., were told to bring " letters of proxy so that whatever the Legate decreed in Council should be esteemed ratified everywhere."

That is what Otho wished. *But nothing like that happened.*

The Prelates when assembled requested Otho to absent himself the first day so that they " might consider his proposals and deliberate lest he should attempt to enact anything to their prejudice." How could they have better safeguarded the independence of their Provincial Synods and have more decisively rejected the jurisdiction of the Pope ?

The King thought it necessary on the second day. to provide a Body Guard for his guest. The King also sent the Count of Lincoln, John, son of Wilfred, and William Rawleigh, Canon of S. Paul's, " on behalf of King and kingdom to prevent the Legate attempting to pass any statute contrary to the royal crown and dignity."

Atho read the Decretals in a clear voice, and at the end of it all, *not the Decretals, but the Constitutions of Otho, were passed, which differ a good deal from the Decretals.*

The Constitutions of Otho are named and dated like every other such Mediæval Document in Ecclesiastical

History by the name of the President, just as an Act of Parliament is dated and named by the name of the Sovereign.

The King exercised a right of veto where the State was concerned.[12] The fact that his three representatives did not exercise that right shows that the King assented.

The *authority of the Constitutions* of Otho was that of the Council which passed them, not of the President; witness the words in which Otho himself promulged the results :

> " Denique nos Otho . . . . astantis Concilii suffragio et consensu . . . . . . "

> " Finally WE, Otho . . . . *by the vote and consent of the present Council* for the strengthening and reforming of the Church in England, without impairing other canonical institutes which we wish and command to be kept with reverence."

There is a gloss on " consensu " by John Atho who was present and was acting as Otho's secretary.

> " It is plain in this passage that Councils of [13]Prelates must be had recourse to in the publication of Constitutions of this kind."

As a fact, there were several differences between these Constitutions and the Decretals, but even if all the Councillors had adopted the Decretals *en bloc* and ignored English customs, still in the face of those records it would have been on *English authority* that the Constitutions of Otho were based.

The Council of Othobon passed canons in much the same way. But their authority being in doubt, they were confirmed by Peccham's Lambeth Council in 1281 which goes to show at the least that *English authority* was considered necessary to their validity.

So we come to the end of the thirteenth century with

---

[12] Sir Lewis Dibdin (Report in *Church and State*, 1916, page 282) denies this on authority of Bishop Stubbs in passage quoted.

[13] " Prelates " is not a synonym for " bishop." It is used in Canon Law correctly as p. pass. participle of " preferro."

English Provincial Councils still paramount after the Canons of the Six General Councils.

This brings us to a period during which no great codification of English Church Law was attempted—the fourteenth and early fifteenth centuries. Questions were dealt with as they arose by various Provincial Synods.

The question has been asked—and sometimes answered in the negative—Did this system of English Canon Law and of Provincial Jurisdiction ever really work?

The answer must be carefully guarded by a caveat.

English Criminal Law had absolutely broken down in the fourteenth and fifteenth centuries; and was practically inoperative. But the use and abuse of the system of Sanctuary through this period proves that the population as a whole felt more security and more likelihood of justice in appealing to the Church than in appealing to the civil courts.

The point is dealt with at some length in a four column leading article in the Literary Supplement of the *Times* for 13th Jan., 1927. The article is based on five prolonged studies :—

> *The Eyre of Kent*, W. C. Bolland. (Selden Society, 28/-.)
>
> *Select Bills in Eyre*, W. C. Bolland. (Selden Society, 28/-.)
>
> *Calendar of Coroner's Rolls of the City of London, 1300—1378*. (R. R. Sharpe, Richard Clay.)
>
> *The Destruction of the Sanctuary*, by Isobel D. Thornley. (Longman's, 15/-.)
>
> *Das Recht im Bilde*. Von Hans Fehr. (Munich, Eugen Reutsch Verlag.)

These led the writer of the article to the conclusion stated above.

Consequently, though the Ecclesiastical Law was more observed and more respected than the Criminal Law which had broken down, we must not expect Ecclesiastical Law to have been working under that handicap with the smooth uniform certainty of enforcement which we now-a-days associate with Criminal Law in England. A further handicap of course was provided by the rival claim to jurisdiction made by the Papacy. A *modus vivendi* was arrived at, but the rival claims were still *sub judice*, as I pointed out in an article in *Theology*, August, 1927.

So the answer to the question, Did English Canon Law and Jurisdiction really work in the fourteenth and early fifteenth century? is, that it did really work as well as it could and that was better than might have been expected. But by 1420 it wanted bringing up to date once more.

That was done by the codification of *English Provincial Canon Law*, by Lyndwood, published in 1432, and that was accepted by both Canterbury and York Convocations. Further, Lyndwood was regarded as the law which should be enforced, during and after the Reformation until constitutionally altered. The proof is that Lyndwood was printed in English in 1534—the year of the Act which provided the method of dealing with Canon Law in future and also gave Lyndwood, until altered, the force of Statute Law.

We must not forget that Henry VIII. had no dispute re doctrine with the Pope who had himself called Henry *Fidei Defensor*. Henry's quarrel was entirely on the question of jurisdiction. He certainly ended the Pope's jurisdiction in this country : and he as certainly vindicated as current the authority of the English Provincial Canons, always assuming that the Canons of the first Four General Councils at least were behind them.

Here is the acceptance of Lyndwood by York Convocation.

Reg. Booth Ebor f342. b.

" Quod praelati et clerus in praedicta convocatione volunt et concedunt unanimiter quod effectus Constitutionum provincialium Cantua rionsium Ante haec tempora tentarum et habitarum *Constitutionibus provinciae eboracensis nullo modo repugnantium seu praejudicialium et non aliter, nec alio modo,* admittantur, et quod hujus modi, constitutiones provinciae eboracensis, prout indiget et decet, inserantur et cum iisdem de cetero incorporentur et pro jure observentur."

The *fact* of the refusal of the two provinces of Canterbury and York to accept the Decretals on Papal authority, and the above passage, answer two of the main arguments in favour of Rome's authority put forward by the late H. W. C. Davis, Professor of Modern History at Oxford, in an article on the Canon Law in England published in *Zeitschrift Der Savigny—Stiftung fur Rechts geschichte* (Weimar Herman Böhlaus Nachfolger, 1913).

Another of Professor Davis' arguments that English Canon Law differed but little from Roman Canon Law is open to question, but it is beside the mark, since the whole question is not as to the content of the Canon Law, but its *authority*.

That brings us to Lyndwood—and here he is in the 1534 translation with only such alterations in spelling and words as seemed necessary to make him easily readable.

William Lyndwood, 1375—1446, educated at Gonville and Caius Coll. Camb: Fellow of Pembroke Hall, removed to Oxford. LL. D.

1414 Official Principal to Archbishop Chichele.

1428 Dean of Arches.

Employed in diplomatic business in Burgundy, Portugal, France, Spain, Scotland, Hanseatic League, during which business at the Archbishop's request he wrote " Provinciale " completed 1433.

1432—3 Keeper of Privy Seal.

1442   Bp. of St. David's.

The book represents the practice of the Court of Arches in his time.

The article on him in Ollard and Crosse is to be read cautiously, as the account of Matthew Paris appears to have been neglected by the writer, who assumes that the authority of the Council of Otho was that of the Legate, whereas it was that of the Council as shewn above.

A similar caution must be used in accepting statements made about Lyndwood by various writers. E.g., Rev. P. G.

Ward, in *Church Times*, Aug. 24th, 1928, says that Lyndwood's last paragraph in his Introduction implies that Provincial constitutions were local supplements of the Corpus Juris Canonici. I cannot find a word in the reference to justify the statement.

c

INTRODUCTION.

II.—By H. C. BELL.

From the beginning of the Reformation onwards, the interest of Lyndwood's *Provinciale* ceases to be academic, and becomes practical. At this point it is necessary for the student to perform a feat of mental gymnastics. Historians, theologians and lawyers alike have shown the greatest reluctance, when dealing with this subject, to cross the boundary which separates the later middle ages from the Reformation period. Canon Law has been treated as belonging properly to European mediæval history, and as touching the history of England as many other features of the general history of Europe touch it, in the character of " outside influences." Canon Law before the Reformation has been regarded as a plant of foreign growth, never very much at home in English soil; and since the Reformation it has been accounted a weed. The few, and they have been very few, who have tried to invest the subject with more than an antiquarian interest, have been dismissed as harmless cranks, as long as they stuck to theory, and treated as dangerous reactionaries if they tried to put their theories into practice. " By what law of the Established Church can you justify this practice? " demanded a Bishop of a clergyman, with whom he had a difference of opinion. " By the Canon Law," the priest replied. " Indeed," said the Bishop, " I did not know that you were as old as that." As a specimen of mild episcopal humour this will pass; it indicates a fairly common attitude.

Before we can attempt to estimate the significance of the *Provinciale* from the point where it was left in the first part of this Introduction, it will be necessary to refer to, and then dismiss finally from our minds, four questions which always loom large in discussions of the subject, and which possess considerable historical interest; but which—and it is this which it is so necessary for the student to realise—are of no practical importance.

The first of these is the question, What is the precise nature of the authority which lay behind the Canon Law in England before the Reformation? This is known as the Stubbs-Maitland controversy. It is a subject of absorbing interest to students of history; so much so, in fact, that it is difficult sometimes to persuade them that there is any other problem at all connected with the Canon Law. No introduction to the *Provinciale* would be complete without some discussion of it, and it has been adequately dealt with in Part I. From now on, it need not concern us. To understand this, is the chief mental somersault to which reference has been made.

The next is the question, What is the actual character of the *Provinciale?* It is probable that the immediate occasion of Lyndwood's work was the attempt made by civil lawyers to apply the Acts of Praemunire (the object of which Acts was to prevent appeals being taken out of this country to Rome), so as to prevent appeals to the provincial courts. This was a distinct misapplication of the statutes, but it is not an uncommon thing for lawyers to apply a statute in a way which its framers never intended. Lyndwood, at the urgent request of Archbishop Chichele, whose chaplain he was, collected and arranged the Provincial Constitutions of the English Church, omitting what he felt to be superfluous, making certain abbreviations, and adding a commentary with the object of strengthening faith, reforming morals, and providing material for the direction of the simple, and the salvation of souls. He was not, of course, the only person who attempted to codify the Canon Law. Whether Lyndwood carried his work through with intention that it should rank as a private collection, with just that degree of authority which his personal reputation could give it, or whether it was intended that some sanction should be sought for it, which would make it an official text-book, whether it did or did not claim to be a complete codex for the English Church, are questions, which, though interesting, do not matter very much. As a matter of fact, it does cover the ground fairly completely. It does not, however, in the least detract from the practical importance which events have given it, to admit for the sake of argument and in order to clear the ground, that it was "merely a private collection."

The third question is, What was Lyndwood's intention in writing his book, and to whom did he expect it to be useful? Maitland says that it was an elementary text-book for beginners. If he means for beginners in the study of the law, one may be allowed to differ. It is too special in its character for that. Law students would cover a far wider ground, and would begin with the recognised books on civil law. It seems fairly clear from what Lyndwood himself says that the inexpert for whom he wrote were the clergy who needed to know what the law was, and needed a handy book of reference. But again let it be said, that whatever the intention, the facts of its after history are not affected.

The fourth question which is often the subject of debate, concerns the exact nature of the "acceptance" of the *Provinciale* by the Convocations. That it was " accepted " is not disputed, but acceptance might range from the formal promulgation of Lyndwood's collection of canons, as the official Canon Law of England, to a general approval of the book, as a book of reference for the English clergy. The whole of the canons contained in the *Provinciale* had, at some time or other, been promulgated by English Synods, as Provincial Constitutions; they were already authoritative and probably few will quarrel with the very careful statement of the York Convocation Committee that " Lyndwood's collection of canons was accepted by both Convocations, as the consolidation of English Canon Law as then practised." But as events turned out, whatever the effect of this acceptance, it only retained its outstanding importance, for reasons which will be explained, for about a hundred years.

Having then cleared the ground, it is possible to go on to consider the foundations for the claim that is here put forward, on behalf of the practical importance of the *Provinciale* since the Reformation, and in our own time.

The first point in establishing this claim will need some explanation by reference to events at the beginning of the movement for reform.

In 1534, Henry VIII. was completing preparations for substituting Royal for Papal supremacy over the Church. He desired to carry the Convocations with him in this. In March, 1532 the Commons formulated a complaint against the clergy to the effect that they claimed to execute canons made by Convocation without the Royal Assent, and also to enact new canons. The complaint was transmitted to Convocation by the King, through Archbishop Warham, on April 12, for consideration and reply.

Convocation replied that they did not think the ground of complaint against the "old" canons, that some of them were contrary to the Royal Prerogative, was well founded, and that probably Parliament had misunderstood the meaning of them. They refused to surrender the right to enact new canons. This reply was not satisfactory to the King, and the question was on April 29 referred back to Convocation for a further answer.

Convocation then replied that if the "old" canons could be shown in any particular to be "contrariant," the parts which so offended should be revoked. New canons should be suspended in their operation pending the Royal Assent. The reply was so cautiously worded, and appeared to leave so many loopholes, that the King still expressed himself dissatisfied.

On May 10 the King sent a form of submission to the Royal authority, which the clergy declined to accept.

On May 15 the King sent a second form which bound the clergy not to "attempt, alledge, claim or put in ure" the "old" canons, and not to "enact, promulge, or execute" any new ones. Convocation accepted the terms "enact, put in ure, promulge, or execute" with regard to new canons, and this document formed the basis of the Act of Submission of 1534.

When the draft of the Act made its appearance, the

distinction between " old " and " new " canons had disappeared. All seven of the above terms were used of new canons, but in such a way that it might be argued that the first four were intended to apply to the " old." These " old " canons were the subject of the chief clauses of the Act of Submission. The question arises, what were these " old " canons?

At this period the *Provinciale* was in the heyday of its reputation. During the preceding forty years one edition had succeeded another; it was the accepted text-book, and the only text-book which was accessible to English churchmen in general. In 1534 there appeared a translation of the canons of the *Provinciale* into English, without Lyndwood's gloss. The issue of the canons by themselves is an indication that they were considered to possess some authority, apart from Lyndwood's commentary on them; but besides this, the English translation bears unmistakable marks of having been inspired.

" Here after ensuen the Constitucions provincialles, and of Otho, and Othobone, whiche be not put forthe to binde any of our moste gracious soveraygne lorde the kynges subiectes, but to the only entent that ye people of this realme of Englande shulde know them, suche as they be. For the Clergy of this realme (whome comenly we have used to call the churche, or the spiritualtie) without thassent of ye kyngs hyghnes, the nobiliti and comens of this realme, have never had, ne yet have any juste and lawful power to make any Constitutions or lawes over any of our sayde soveraygne lorde the Kyngs subiectes."

The language of this preface is very similar to that used by the King in his communications to Convocation, and to the wording of the Act of Submission itself.

Moreover, a study of the " translatour's " words " to the readers," reveals that while he was considering how best to counteract the influence of the Lutheran heresy, " there came one and desyred me in his name that might upon my dewty have commaunded me, to take the paynes to translate in to Englyshe the Constitutions provinciall . . . ." These Constitutions he repeatedly speaks of as " the olde doctrine " and " olde lernynge." It was, evidently, felt in exalted quarters that a reprint of Lyndwood's canons in English was advisable in view of probable developments.

This is the first point, and the first step in the history of this work, as a document of practical importance to the English Church at the present time. It is to the canons of the *Provinciale* that the provisions of the Act of Submission refer.

The next stage is to consider the effect upon the *Provinciale* of the Act of Submission of the Clergy of 1534. The Act consists of seven clauses. Four of these, 1, 2, 3 and 7, are concerned with the revision of the Canon Law. The other three clauses, 4, 5 and 6, deal with a different subject, the restraint of appeals to Rome.

A bill, embodying clauses 1, 2 and 3, was submitted to Convocation for approval. This bill, and the eventual act, after reciting the necessity for revision of the law, provides for the appointment of a Commission, consisting of thirty-two persons, of whom sixteen were to be chosen from the House of Lords, and sixteen from the Commons. The Commission was to be charged with the task of reviewing the old canons, and deciding which of them should be abrogated, and which retained in force. To these latter the King's assent is to be given, and they are to stand in their full strength and power.

The third clause provides that no new canons shall be enacted by Convocation without the Royal Assent. As long ago as 1532, when the articles to which reference has been made above were before Convocation, some anxiety seems to have been felt over the vagueness as to the date of appointment of the promised Commission. When the articles were voted upon by the Upper House, two Bishops made reservations on this point. In the event, this anxiety was justified, for the Commission was never appointed. It is possible that Henry never intended that it should be appointed, and the course of events suggests that the Bishops may have had reasons to suspect this. Convocation took the precaution of adding a clause to the bill now presented to them. This is clause 7 of the Act, and according to the printed Statutes of the Realm, III., 461, it was " inserted on a schedule annexed to the original Act." The Bill, with this added clause, concludes with the note " à cette provision les Communes sont assentez." Fortunately, it does not matter now, though it is interesting to speculate on how this clause obtained the Royal Assent. The King, at that time, may have intended that the Commission should be appointed, and do its work. He may have made a slip, to which even clever men are liable, and accepted the clause without appreciating the extent to which it modified all that had gone before, or he may have thought it wisest to say nothing, and trust to dealing in a " tudoresque " manner with the situation when it arose. The clergy had not shown themselves too amenable in the matter of the Submission, and Henry was anxious to gain his main point.

The clause is of vital importance, for it provides for the period intervening between the passing of the Act, and the appointment of the Commission, and since the Commission has never been appointed, the clause is still in operation.

It runs as follows : " Provyded also that suche canons, constitucions ordynaunces and synodals provynciall being allredy made, which be not contraryant nor repugnant to the lawes, statutes and customes of this realme nor to the damage or hurte of the Kynges prerogatyve royall, shall nowe styll be used and executed as they were afore the makyng of this Acte, tyll suche tyme as they be vyewed serched or otherwyse ordered and detmyned by the seid XXXIJ persons or the more parte of theym, according to the tenour fourme, and effecte of this present Acte."

The effect of this is that the Canon Law as practised in England, so far as it did not run counter to the laws of the realm as they were in 1534, remains in force at the present time, except where it has been deliberately repealed, pending the appointment of the Commission named in the Act for its revision. That is our second point in estimating the practical value of the

Provinciale, as the foundation of the existing law of the Church of England.

At this stage there is another matter to be considered. The post-Reformation period has witnessed a gradual encroachment made by the legal profession on the rights of the Church. With the increasing tendency of the State to legislate for the Church without her consent, the habit grew up of interpreting this clause of the Act of Submission, as if it meant that the Canon Law was to be modified automatically so that it was not "contraryant nor repugnant" to any civil legislation since 1534. It is significant that in the edition of the Statutes of the Realm issued at the beginning of the eighteenth century, the clause is made to read, "which *shall not* be contraryant nor repugnant, etc." This falsifying of the text fitted in with the practice of the civil lawyers at the time. It is arrived at by transferring the words of clause 3 of the Act, which refers to the enactment of new canons, to clause 7 which refers to those canons "allredy made."

Two comments may be made upon this. "Contraryant" and "repugnant" are not the same thing as "different from." There is nothing to prevent the Church having a stricter rule for its members, as for example, in the matter of marriage, than is provided for by State law. It is altogether a different thing for the Church to say that you may not marry your deceased wife's sister, while the State says that you may, from what it is for the Church to say that you may do so, when the State says that you may not. In the former case the law is "different," in the second it is "contraryant."

And further, the actual meaning of the clause is made clear by the preamble to the Royal Licence issued to Convocation in 1865, to amend certain of the canons of 1604. This preamble indicates the distinction between existing and new canons, as regards their relation to the Statute Law.

" By the said act (the Act of Submission) it is provided that no Canons, Constitutions or Ordinances shall be made or put in execution within this realm by authority of the

Convocations of the Clergy, which *shall be* contrariant or repugnant . . . . etc."

" And lastly it is also provided by the said act that such Canons, Constitutions, Ordinances, and Synodals Provincial which were then already made, and which *were not* contrary or repugnant . : . . etc."

This, surely, finally settles the question of the interpretation of the Act of 1534.

This leads to the question, By what means can alterations in the Canon Law have been effected since the acceptance of the *Provinciale* by the Convocation of York in 1462? (It had been accepted by Canterbury earlier.)

Clause 7 of the Act of Submission excludes from continuance any canons, which ran counter to the laws of the realm or to the Royal Prerogative. The canonical enactments which were affected by this are few and unimportant. Between 1462 and 1534 seventeen statutes were passed dealing with ecclesiastical matters. Of these, five are concerned with Benefit of Clergy; four with Probate; one protects ordinaries who punish " incontinent priests " from process in the civil courts; one allows the marriage of Chancery clerks " after the laws of Holy Church "; one makes prison breaking by clerks a felony; one deals with pluralities, and one with land given " to the use of " a Church; one gives a general pardon to those who have infringed the anti-papal statutes in the past; and the remaining two are the Reformation statutes of Citations and Appeals.

Benefit of Clergy and Probate are referred to below. For the rest, anything in these statutes which is found to conflict with Canon Law must be held to modify it.

Next, the Canon Law can be modified by Acts of Parliament passed since 1534 with the consent of Convocation, and by Canons which have received the Royal Assent.

Changes under this head are much less extensive than is commonly supposed. During the periods 1689—1700, and 1717—1850, the Convocations did not transact business. During those periods no alteration can have taken place in the Canon Law. In the Act of Submission the restriction on the making of canons without the Royal Assent is stated clearly enough. It is not so clearly laid down that Parliament could not amend the law of the Church without the consent of Convocation, but it is implied. Convocation was recognised as an integral part of the constitution.

The supremacy of statute law goes without saying. Parliament, as long as it has the support of the country, can deal as it likes with any institution in the country. It can force the Church of England to admit to Communion persons who have broken the Church's laws of marriage, and it can imprison priests who refuse to obey its injunctions. It can make communists eligible for membership of the Carlton Club, and could imprison a Committee which refused to accept their nominations. Both proceedings would be tyranny, and bad government, but there is no question about the power of Parliament to do either. Interference by the State with the intimate affairs of the Church, without her consent, involves a denial to one institution in the country of rights which are freely granted to all other institutions, and is a departure from the bargain made at the Reformation. The phrase about " undoing the work of the Reformation " is familiar in another connection. It might well be borne in mind by those who are fondest of using the phrase, that there are more ways than one of going behind the Reformation Settlement.

In considering possible modifications under this head, therefore, we are entitled to regard the consent of Convocation, as an essential element, side by side with the Royal Assent.

But it is necessary to distinguish different degrees of approval by Convocation. If we are to rule out everything that has not been formally sanctioned, we shall have to exclude probably the Prayer Book of 1549, and certainly those of 1552 and 1559. But the last of these was accepted in practice and acted upon. It might be argued that State legislation which has been received by the Church and acted upon without protest, and which does not infringe any principle, is to be regarded as having received a general sanction. But this could not extend to detail, and could not be sustained as regards a practice which definitely conflicted with a provision of the Canon Law.

For example, the absence of any mention of Reservation of the Blessed Sacrament in 1559 might he held to protect a priest who did not reserve from the imputation of illegal action, but it could not lay open to a charge of illegality a priest who did continue to carry out the directions of the *Provinciale, Book III. Tit. 25, chap. 2.*

When the task of consolidating the Canon Law is undertaken, it will be found that the amount of deliberate amendment which has taken place since the Reformation is small. The question of the interpretation of rubrics will be considered later.

We pass to alterations which have come about through portions of the Canon Law becoming obsolete.

Reference was made above to an Act of Parliament which restricted Benefit of Clergy. Benefit of Clergy was a privilege granted by the State and liable to be withdrawn. While it existed, it was necessary that rules for its use should be put forth by the Church. It is no principle of Christianity that ecclesiastical persons should be subject to a different procedure from other citizens, when accused of offences against the civil government. When the State chose to withdraw the privilege, the canons on the subject ceased to be operative. They were not repealed, but the conditions in which they applied, and over which the Church had no control, no longer existed. Benefit of Clergy finally came to an end in 1828.

Another instance is Probate. All dealings with testamentary matters were formerly the business of the Church Courts. In a Christian State there is something to be said for this arrangement, in a neutral State there is none. The subject of testaments is not one which the conscience of Christians can only allow to be dealt with under Church Law, and it is no real part of the work of the clergy. The canons which lay down principles to guide the testamentary dispositions of Churchmen continue to make their appeal to the conscience, but except in a Christian State they could not be enforced, and if they could, the wisdom of enforcing them is questionable.

Notice should be taken of those parts of the Canon Law which have fallen into disuse. Disuse, by the way, is not the same thing as the very technical process known as " desuetude." Disuse alone cannot abrogate a canon.

The canons concerning Regulars for instance, are not obsolete, but fell into disuse because the class of persons to whom they applied ceased to exist. Strictly speaking, the revival of the monastic orders automatically revives the canons which apply to them. They certainly badly need revision, but in the meantime there is no question about their being in force.

So with ceremonies which have fallen into disuse, and have not been actually abolished. However long they may be in abeyance, as soon as they are revived they must be performed in the manner and with the accessories laid down in the canons.

Desuetude, and the establishment of contrary custom, is a well known principle of Canon Law, and opens up a large question.

Under certain circumstances a provision of the Canon Law may be set aside by being disused, and by the establishment of a new custom contrary to the law. The abrogation of a canon by this means is hedged round with many restrictions, one of the most important being the necessity for proof that the change is productive of good in the region both of faith and morals. The appeal to desuetude is the last ditch in which they entrench themselves who wish to relegate the *Provinciale* to the position of a mediæval document, of no practical value at the present day. " Even if you *can* prove that the Canon Law has never been repealed, it has been abrogated long ago by desuetude."

Here arises a point which up to the present has escaped notice. Since 1534 the Canon Law in the English Church has not been subject as regards amendment and repeal to the rules which govern Canon Law in general, but is subject to a procedure of its own, which is regulated by statute. Amendment is to be made after recommendations of a Commission of thirty-two persons who are to be appointed for the purpose. Until that Commission reports, no change is to be made. This cannot prevent amendment or repeal by subsequent statute with consent of Convocation, for no statute can bind future statutes, but it does do away altogether with the operation of desuetude, which has never applied to statute law.

It is particularly interesting to hear this argument from desuetude advanced by persons who in the ordinary way never hesitate to exalt the statute law at the expense of the law of the Church.

We have now to deal with the claim that the Canon Law is modified by the Rubrics of the Book of Common Prayer. The question may be put in the well known form " When is a rubric not a rubric? " The answer is, that since 1874 rubrics have been regarded by the civil courts as having the force of law as if they were clauses in a statute, and have been interpreted in the same way as an Act of Parliament.

A rubric is originally a direction for the conduct of divine service, and presupposes a knowledge of the principles upon which the liturgy is constructed, and some knowledge also of the Canon Law which lies behind it. The relation of a rubric to a canon is very much that of a bye-law to an Act of Parliament. It is limited in its application, and if, accidentally or otherwise, it runs counter to the wider law, it has no validity as against that law. Rubrics must always be interpreted in the light of canons, and not canons in the light of rubrics.

The Prayer Book provides a few interesting exceptions to this definition. The most noteworthy are the " Black Rubric " and the statement about the certainty of salvation of baptised infants. Both these deal with doctrinal subjects which are outside the province of rubrics altogether. Others appear to go outside their proper sphere, though they are actually drawing attention to canonical injunctions which affect the use of a service. Such are the rubric restricting the use of the burial service, and that on the use of the sign of the cross.

Before a rubric can be held to have modified a canon, it must be shown that the rubric was drawn up with that deliberate intention, and was promulgated by the competent authority.

How do the successive Prayer Books stand as regards this?

The books of 1552 and 1559 did not receive the consent of Convocation, and possess no definite canonical authority. The book of 1559 must, however, be held to possess such authority as it could acquire by being brought into use without protest, but that amounts to nothing when it is a question of the abrogation of canons. The book of 1549 may have received the consent of Convocation. As is well known, the records of Convocation for that period were destroyed in the great Fire of London, and the only evidence is a letter from the Council to Bonner. Bishop Stubbs believed that the book did receive the approval of Convocation. But there is a doubt, and there is still greater uncertainty about the intentions of Convocation, if the book were approved. Where it is at all possible to make the directions of the book square with the canons, there would seem to be no justification for any other course.

When we come to the book of 1662 the position is different. That book was approved by Convocation, and in circumstances which go to show that all that the Church did, it did deliberately. The revisers of 1662 had taken part in the Savoy Conference two years previously. They understood better than any of their predecessors the nature of the task upon which they were engaged. They realised the condition of religious feeling in England at the time, and the limitations which it placed upon their work. In a marked way they provided for a state of things which did not obtain at the moment, but which might come to pass, when the background of the Canon Law came to be properly understood.

The best example is the Ornaments Rubric. The rubric of 1559 was retained, in spite of all the protests made at the Savoy Conference, and the standard of ceremonial remained that of the period just before the first Prayer Book. This was the standard of the *Provinciale*. The only accessories of worship of which it can be said with certainty, that they were retained and in use by the authority of Parliament in the second year of Edward VI., are those set out in the inventory in *Provinciale* III., Tit. 27, chap. 2. The majority of these ornaments were not being used, had not been for many years, and as far as anyone could have seen, were not likely to be. Yet the order for their use was made.

Now it is a fact of the greatest significance that within a few years a new edition of the *Provinciale* was issued, the first since the early days of the sixteenth century. This was by no means a mere exhibition of archæological zeal. The new edition has the contractions of the old Latin text expanded; it possesses copious indexes and summaries, and the editor's preface states that it is intended for practical use, as it contains "the whole marrow of the law." It is significant, too, in this connection, that its publication was followed in a few years by the appearance of the corrupt text of the Act of Submission, the use of which enabled the secular lawyers to discount the value of the *Provinciale*.

One more point remains to be mentioned. The Canons of 1604 present a difficulty. They do not possess the same authority in the Province of York as they do in that of Canterbury, for the Convocation of York only "assented" to them, and that under duress. Strictly, they have no canonical authority in the North. With regard to the canons themselves, the position is summed up in a sentence from the York Convocation Committee's report on the Canon Law. "In practice, these canons do not greatly affect the law. In some respects they aim at

D

bringing existing canons up to date; they set a minimum
standard in public worship which the circumstances of the
time called for; in any consolidation of Canon Law, it
would be found that they belonged rather conspicuously
to the age which produced them, and what was of
permanent value would naturally be cast in more modern
form."

For the sake of clearness it will be as well to summarise
the conclusions at which we have arrived.

    1. It is to the *Provinciale* that the term " the old
Canons " in the Act of Submission refers.

    2. Clause 7 of that Act is still operative, and all the
canons of the *Provinciale* are in force, except—

        A. Those which conflict with the law of the realm
as it was in 1534.

        B. Those which have been abrogated since.

    3. The means by which abrogation can take place are—

        A. By Act of Parliament which has been " con-
sented " to by Convocation.

        B. By Canon which has received the Royal Assent.

        C. By Canons becoming obsolete, through radical
change of circumstances, but *not*—

            (a.) Through " desuetude."

            (b.) By the discovery that the strict observ-
ance of a rubric is inconsistent with a
Canon.

This translation of the *Provinciale* is commended to the
clergy and others, in the hope that in course of time it
may form the basis of a consolidation of English Church
Law, and the production of a complete codex. Nobody
would suggest that the *Provinciale* as it stands is a satisfactory text book of ecclesiastical law for use in the
Church to-day. It is out of date and, like the Book of
Common Prayer, unsuited to the needs of this generation.
But like the Book of Common Prayer it is authoritative
in its own sphere. It needs revision, but again, like the
Book of Common Prayer, it is not properly revised by
being ignored. That has been the practice of the courts
for the last fifty years.

One thing stands out as of urgent necessity. A clean sweep must be made of all the judgments of the Court of Arches and the Privy Council since 1874. Those judgments have lost all the repute they ever possessed, and are not likely to be made the basis of new ones, but that is not sufficient. The possibility of their use must be prevented. One instance will show the kind of thing from which the Church needs to be protected.

The *Provinciale* enacts that there shall be two lights, or at least one, on the Altar at the time of the celebration of the Eucharist. In 1877 the Privy Council ruled that lights on the Altar, except for the purpose of giving light, were illegal. Yet nothing had happened since 1534 to vary the canon. The point came up again in the Lincoln Case. The Archbishop pronounced lights to be legal. On appeal, the Privy Council shirked the issue, but hinted that had they been obliged to decide the point, they might have been influenced by the Archbishop's judgment. In 1920, the matter came up again in the King's Bench. The judge ignored the Lincoln judgment altogether, and the whole of the previous history of the question, and decided that Altar Lights were illegal, because the Privy Council had pronounced them to be illegal in 1877.

The business of reforming the Church Courts is shortly to be undertaken. If that important work is to be brought to a successful issue, it will need to be done side by side with the revision of the law, for experience shows that the difficulty of the Church Courts, is not only a matter of personnel and procedure, but is connected with the doubtful character of the law administered in them. Amidst all her troubles the greatest hope of peace for the Church of England, is in the possession of a body of law, of unquestionable authority, which is easily accessible to everybody, and which everybody can understand.

THE FIRST BOOK.

TITULUS 1.
Of The Most High Trinity and the Catholic Faith.

CHAPTER I.   Summary.

All Ministers of the Church are bound to know and to believe the 14 Articles of the Catholic Faith of which 7 appertain and belong to the Mystery of the Holy Trinity and the other 7 to the Humanity of Christe, as in this Constitution and Decree is rehearsed.

Ignorantia sacerdotum.   Canon of John Peccham.

That no person may excuse himself by ignorance but that he know the Articles of the faith which all ministers of the Church be bound to know, we shortly and briefly touch and rehearse them in manner and form as here followeth. For it is to be known that there be 7 Articles of the Faith appertaining to the Mystery of the Trinity of which 7 four appertain and belong to the privities of the divinity or Godhead of the same Trinity and three belong to the effects, that is to say the operation of God.

The first Article is the Unity of the Essence of God, that is to say, that there is none but one God in an indivisible and inseparable Trinity of Three Persons, according to the First Article of the Creed *Credo in Unum Deum*, that is to say in English " I believe in One God."

The Second Article is to believe the Father unbegotten, being of Himself and not of any other to be God.

The Third is to believe the Son of God Only-begotten to be God.

The Fourth is to believe the Holy Ghost to be God, being neither Begotten nor un-begotten but proceeding together and equally from both the Father and the Son.

1

The Fifth is the Creation of Heaven and of Earth, that is to say, of all and every Creature both visible and invisible by the whole indivisible Trinity.

The Sixth is the Sanctification and hallowing of the Church by the Holy Ghost, and the Sacraments of Grace and all other things in which the *Church of Christ* doth common and participate; wherein is understood that the said Church with her sacraments and laws through the Holy Ghost is sufficient, for and unto everyman how great a sinner soever he be, for his salvation; and that out of this Church is no Health of salvation.

The Seventh is the Consummation of the same Church, militant, by eternal glory certainly to be suscitate and raised in flesh or body and soul; and by the contrary of this is understood the eternal damnation of evil persons refused of God.

The other Seven Articles appertain to the Humanity or Manhood of Christ.

The First is the Incarnation or true assumption and taking of man's flesh and body of the glorious Virgin only by the Holy Ghost.

The Second is the Nativity of God truly and verily Incarnate of a virgin, pure clean and undefiled.

The Third is the true Passion and Death of Christ upon the Cross under the tyrant Pilate.

The Fourth is the Descension and going down of Christ to Hell in His soul (His body remaining and lying in the sepulchre), to spoil and destroy Hell, that is to deliver the souls of the Holy Fathers there lying and abiding redemption.

The Fifth is the true Resurrection and again rising of Christ.

The Sixth is the true Ascension of the same Christ to Heaven.

The Seventh is the most sure, certain and undoubted expectation, and looking for the same Christ to come to judge both quick and dead.

CHAPTER II.   Summary.

They that minister the Body of our Lord must teach
and inform them unto whom they do minister that under
the form of bread is Very Christ, and that He ought to
be received comely and seemingly; and that under the
form of wine, being given not before consecrate, is but
wine only and nothing else.

Altissimus et infra.   Canon of John Peccham.

The Priests ought to take heed that when they give or
minister the communion of the Holy Sacrament to the
simple folk in the Easter Season or elsewhere, that they
teach and inform them curiously and substantially that in
form of bread is given and ministered unto them both the
Body and the Blood of our Lord, yea and very Christ
Holy and Alive, Which is there whole under the form of
the Sacrament.

They ought also to teach the same simple, rude and
unlearned folk, that that which at the same time is given
and ministered in the Chalice not to be any Sacrament,
but pure wine only given to them to drink that they may
the more easily and sooner swallow down the Sacrament
which they have received; for in such inferior churches,
that is to say churches or chapels of the country, yea, and
parish churches of the City or any other churches being
not Cathedral churches it is permitted and granted only
to them that do celebrate to receive the Blood of Christ
under the form of wine consecrate. Let them also teach
the same rude and simple folk not to break over small
nor too much with their teeth the same Holy Sacrament
received with their mouth, but the same very little broken
whole to take and swallow down perfectly that no little
part or piece thereof perchance remain between the teeth
or elsewhere.

4   Lyndwood's Provinciale

TITULUS 2.
Of Constitutions.

CHAPTER I.   Summary.

*That the Constitution made and ordained against con-
cubinaries be kept inviolably and in the most strait way;
and the same Constitution to be denounced and published
by the officials in four principal chapters rural.*

Quia incontinentiae vicium et infra.

Canon of John Peccham.

We bid and command the Constitution of the late lord
Othobonus published and made against concubinaries to
be inviolably observed and kept.   And we, straitly enjoining, charge and command *(praecipimus)* all and
every our Lord Bishops and Suffragans, in the virtue of
obedience and under the pain of suspension from their
office and from their benefice (which suspension we pronounce on them if they or any of them shall be found
willingly negligent on this behalf), that they cause the
Constitution afore named to be recited and rehearsed and
openly in the four principal chapters rural of the year,
either by themselves or by their officials or at the least wise
by the deans rural or their deputies before all the chapter,
excluding thence and separating all lay persons; which
recitation or rehearsal we will and command to be had
and taken for a monition, that process may be freely had
and made against all such vicious concubinaries; that
after the said recitation they may have no excuse to lay
for them, when process shall be made against them for
and concerning the execution of privation of their benefices, according to the effect of the sentence and decree
made in the constitution aforesaid.

But if any person or persons shall maliciously let the
said recitation of this constitution aforesaid they shall
immediately for so doing be excommunicate and
accursed; and if any dean or deputy shall be negligent to
recite the said constitution as aforesaid he shall be bound

to fast bread and water every Friday (except infirmity and sickness shall let him) until such time as he shall have recited, or caused to be recited, the said Constitution in the Chapter then next following.

CHAPTER II.   Summary.

Of the custom of the habit and apparel comely and seeming for clerks to wear; commanding the observation and keeping of the same, under the pain constitute and set upon the same.

Exterior habitus et infra.   Canon of John Stratford.

By the authority of this Council we command *(praecipimus)* that the Ordinaries of places, unto whom it belongeth to enquire of the excesses of the subjects, make inquisition and search yearly in all places being subject unto their jurisdiction, by themselves or by other, for and upon the observation of that Constitution made and published by us of the habit, dress and apparel of clerks, and that they see and cause with all diligence to be observed, kept and executed, against all transgressors and offenders on this behalf, the same Constitution upon the pains and penalties in the same Constitution limited.

CHAPTER III.   Summary.

That these Constitutions be diligently to be observed and kept and faithfully published and declared.

Huius autem consilii.   Canon of John Stratford.

We charge and command *(praecipimus)* the Constitutions and remedies provided by this Council to be inviolably observed and kept in this our Province of Canterbury; commanding all our Lord Bishops and Suffragans that they publish and declare and cause to be published and declared and to be brought to every body's knowledge, by themselves or by other, as the law doth require these Constitutions, for the common profit and the laud and glory of the Name of Jesu Christ.

TITULUS 3.
Of Custom.

Chapter I.   Summary.

*Albeit by the old Constitution only the husband, if he
have continued master and owner of three living beasts
or more, and the wife, if she have kept and guided her
household by the space of one whole year, was bound to
the solution and payment of a mortuary,[1] yet now both,
being owner of three or fewer, shall be judged to pay a
mortuary by the Ordinaries of the places.*

Statutum et infra.   Canon of Simon Langham.

Because by the occasion of this statute often times do
arise contention and debate between the parsons of
churches and their parishioners, which strife and debate
we entirely desire to extinguish and put away, we thought
necessary to declare *(illud duximus interpretatione declarandum)* the same statute or custom by Synodal interpretation, expounding the same in this our general
Convocation, to be understood in this manner and form
following, that is to say, if the person deceased have or
had, at the time of his decease, in his goods three live
beasts or more (of whatsoever kind) they be that then
the principal beast reserved to that party unto whom of
right it is owing, the second beast of the said three or
more living beasts be reserved unto that his parish church,
of the which by his life time he received the benefit of the
Sacraments, for and recompense and satisfaction of such
tithes and offerings as he hath taken or kept from the
said parson; and the same after the death of any such
layman to be delivered to his said parish church without
any manner of fraud, guile, deceit, craft or collusion and
without any contradiction or denying, for the health of
the said party's soul. But if there shall be in the goods
of such party so deceasing only two living beasts and no
more, then of the gentle courtesy of the Church all such
action as is in the name or title of a mortuary must be
remitted; and that, if any woman so decease her husband

surviving and remaining in life, in no wise a mortuary be paid for her. But if the woman survive her husband and after his decease continue and remain widow keeping and guarding her household for the space of one year, that then she be bound to pay a mortuary, in manner and form as beforesaid. But yet we will in no wise by this interpretation any prejudice to grow unto the laudable custom and usage heretofore used and kept in this our Province for and concerning mortuaries; but if the party or parties deceasing as aforesaid have the full number of such living beasts, whether the husband or the wife decease before or after, the custom and usage of the church concerning the giving and performing of the mortuary be observed and kept.

And to the payment of the said mortuary due by law or custom we will all such parties as shall refuse, withstand, or gainsay the same, by the Ordinaries of places to be constrained by the censures of the Church.

CHAPTER II.[2]   Summary.

No Parson of any church presume to sell the tithes of his church not yet perceived.

Nullus Rector.   Canon of Edmund.

No Parson may presume to sell the tithes of his church not perceived[a] before the Feast of the Annunciation of the Blessed Virgin Mary, from which day the fruits ought *by custom* to be given to pay the debts or legacies of their persons if they die before the perception of the same fruits.

TITULUS 4.

CHAPTER I.   Summary.

Of the times of giving orders and the quality of persons to be admitted to Orders that unlawfully begotten, having no lawful dispensation, and ordained of any other

[a] Collected in full.

*Bishops than their own, or being in deadly sin, be sus-
pended from the execution of their office until satisfaction be made thereof.*

Eos qui de non legitimo.   Canon of the same Edmund.

Those which be not born in lawful matrimony and
without sufficient dispensation have been promoted to take
Orders, and those also which be not promoted to Holy
Orders by their Bishops and without the licence of their
Bishops or Prelates, we do suspend from the execution of
their order so taken until such time as they have got the
pardon of dispensation.

We do also decree *(decernimus)* that those which take
upon them Holy Orders being in deadly sin committed
before the taking of the same or only for worldly lucre
shall not execute their office, without they be first cleansed
from the same sin by the Sacrament of Penance.

CHAPTER II.   Summary.

*That all irregulars be suspended from the execution of
their office until they have a lawful dispensation.*

In primis et infra.   Canon of the same Edmund.

All those which be irregular, when they do take Orders,
or before or after their Orders taking, without they be
expressly dispensed with by them which may dispense
with such, we denounce *(denuntiamus)* them to be suspended from the executing of their office until such time
as they be lawfully dispensed with for the same.

And as concerning the premises, those which be
irregular be these following :—

Murderers or man killers, advocates in cause of blood,
or simoniacs and interveners or brokers of simoniacal
covenants or bargains, or whosoever wittingly doth take
Orders of them that be infected with that contagion of
simony, or whosoever wittingly doth receive Orders of
heretics, schismatics or by name excommunicate. Also
bigamists, husbands of women actually corrupt before

they were married and such as do corrupt virgins professed into religion or consecrate to God, excommunicate persons and such as by stealth take Orders, soothsayers or prophesyers and burners of churches, and such like folk.

CHAPTER III.   Summary.

Let no man be admitted to Orders out of his own Diocese, of not his own Bishop wittingly.

Quia quidam et infra.   Canon of Richard.

A Bishop, being under our jurisdiction, which shall wittingly give Orders to the clerk or parishioner of another Bishop without the special licence of the same Bishop, from the time of the giving of the same Orders, at which time he received or admitted to Orders any such person until he hath made condign satisfaction, let him know himself to be suspended.

CHAPTER IV.   Summary.

A Prelate shall not cause any of his subjects to be admitted to Orders of not their own Bishop without Letters Dimissory.

Cum quanta et infra.   Canon of Walter.

We do forbid *(prohibemus)* that no Abbot or Prior cause their monks or canons to take Orders of any other Bishop than of the Diocesan of the place without the Letters Dimissory of the same Bishop, or in his absence of his Vicar General.

TITULUS 5.

ONE CHAPTER.   Summary.

Of scrutiny or inquisition to be made at the giving of Orders that no person come to the giving of Orders without diligent scrutiny or examination.

Cum quanta et infra.   Canon of Walter.

No man may come to Orders, or be admitted to the
same, without he have been canonically examined; and
all such clerks as be under the Order of subdeacon shall
not be admitted to the inferior degrees without they have
convenient presentors and be by their testimony admitted.
Also no simoniac, murderer, excommunicate person,
usurer, he that hath committed sacrilege, a burner of
churches, or counterfeiter of writings, or any other
having canonical impediment, shall not presume to come
to any manner of Orders, nor shall be presented or admitted to the same in any wise.

TITULUS 6.

CHAPTER I. Summary.

*Of Holy Unction. . . . . The Archdeacon must take
good heed and beware that no holy or sanctified thing be
put to any profane use.*

Panni chrysmales. Canon of Edmund.

The Chrysmal clothes shall not be turned into any other
use but to the use of the ornaments of the Church, and
likewise other ornaments that be blessed of the Bishops
may not be deputed by any manner of means into profane
uses; and the Archdeacon in his Visitation shall diligently enquire whether this be observed and kept.

CHAPTER II. Summary.

*The Sacrament of Confirmation must be ministered
comely and alone as may be, without intervention of the
parents, or of the father-in-law, or of the mother-in-law.*

Sacerdotes et infra. Canon of Walter.

A young man of the age of 14 years and above to be
confirmed must be monished by the priest of the place
whereas he dwelleth, first to be confessed; and so afterwards must be confirmed, and must come fasting[3] to
confirmation for the reverence of the Sacrament. Also
let the parents be often times warned by the priests that

they bring their young children which be baptised to Confirmation, and that they do not long abide the coming of
the Bishop, but that they bring their children to him for
Confirmation when they shall hear him to be near hand,
and that they bring with them convenient Bishop-bonds.[4]

And the young children also being confirmed, the third
day after their Confirmation must be brought to the
Church and their foreheads must be washed by the hands
of the priests at the font for the reverence of the Chrysm;
and in the same place their bishopbonds then together
must be burnt.

And that at the Confirmation no child be holden of
the father or mother, stepfather or stepmother. And we
will that this prohibition be often published by the priests
in the churches, that the parents and other which do hold
children to the confirming may know that a spiritual bond
is as well contracted and made by this Sacrament as by
Baptism.

CHAPTER III.   Summary.

*All Christians of the age of 14 years or above should
be exhorted to receive the Sacrament of the last anoiling[5]
comely and in due time.*

Cum magna reverentia.   Canon of the same Walter.

The oil of the sick folks shall be brought to the sick
with great reverence : and the priests shall anoint them
with it, with great devotion and solemnity of many
prayers which he ordained for the same. Let the priests
also monish the people, at the least those which be of 14
years and above, to receive the Sacrament of extreme
unction; and that after they have received the sacrament
they may lawfully return to matrimonial copulation.

The effect and virtue of this Sacrament is known by
the words of the Apostle James, saying : " If any of you
be diseased let him bring in the priests of the Church that
they may pray over him, anointing him with the holy oil
in the name of the Lord and the prayer of faith shall save

the diseased and the Lord shall alleviate him, make him light or help him and if he be in sins they shall be forgiven him." (Jas. 5¹⁴.)

CHAPTER IV.   Summary.

The ministers of the Holy Chrysm asking and requiring every year the same Chrysm every year new of their Bishop ought to minister the same duly.

Cum sacri chrysmatis.   Canon of John Peccham.

Whereas the making of the holy ointment is to be done from year to year by the Bishop of the Diocese after the decrees of the holy Canons, the same Chrysm by them made every year is to be given to faithful persons, and the old or whatsoever is left of the old Chrysms is to be burnt in the Churches. The persons also, either by themselves or by their deacons or subdeacons, are bound for every of their churches to ask of the Bishops of their Dioceses the holy Chrysm every year before the Feast of Easter or as shortly as it may be done; insomuch that, if any attempt to christen or to anoint the christened in the forehead (without it be in jeopardy of death) with any other Chrysm than this new which he hath received of the free grant or gift of the Bishop, he sheweth himself to have the sentence of damnation given over him. Yet nevertheless some men being led with blind ignorance (which is said to be very nigh neighbour to deceit) or with a stubborn spirit striving against the holy canons in that behalf (which thing is not far from the crime of idolatry or the sin of witchcraft), do keep in some places the holy Chrysm two years, somewhere three years and more, and do damnably abuse the same in their Christenings and other sacrifices, not asking nor receiving of the Bishops of their Dioceses any new: which thing, lest it should be from henceforth done any more, we straitly command *(praecipimus)* under pain of suspension which we give upon all those stubborn persons that will do the contrary: which thing also we believe ought to be taken and understood of the holy oil of them that be catechumeni, that is to say, newly instructed in the Faith of Christ to be christened.

Chapter V. Summary.

No man ought to be received to the Sacrament of the Altar, but in the article and point of death, except he be confirmed or have lawful impediment.

Confirmationis et infra. Canon of John Peccham.

Against them that be negligent to receive the Sacrament of Confirmation we ordain *(statuimus)* that no man be admitted to the Sacrament of the Body and Blood of our Lord, but in the point of death, without he be confirmed, or except he have been reasonably letted from receiving the said Confirmation.

TITULUS 7.

Of the Iteration of Sacraments, to be done or not done. . . .

Chapter I. Summary.

Let the parents beware that they suffer not their children to be twice confirmed forasmuch as thereby the men children do incur irregularity and the parents' selves great hurt.

Sacerdotes et infra. Canon of Walter.

Let the parents diligently beware and take heed that they bring not their children to be confirmed twice, forasmuch as the same children, by receiving of the same Sacrament again, if they be men children, be made irregular, and the parents' selves by such negligence, by sentence of the Canons, be under great vengeance and punishment.

Chapter II. Summary.

Extreme Unction or Last Anointing ought not to be iterate or given again but one whole year passed between and not then but in evident peril of death.

Sacramentum extremae. Canon of Walter.

E

The Sacrament of Extreme Unction may be lawfully every year renewed, so that every year once it may be given to a person being in great disease and sickness, of the which sickness the sick man is in jeopardy and peril of death.

CHAPTER III.   Summary.

Also Baptism duly ministered by lay persons is not to be iterate, renewed, or ministered again by a priest.

Quod in constitutione et infra. Canon of John Peccham.

If it chance young children to be baptised of lay persons because of peril of death, let the priests beware that they be not so bold to renew the Baptism duly and lawfully done and ministered.

CHAPTER IV.   Summary.

Of the Seven Sacraments of Grace five must and ought to be duly received of all Christian men, which be Baptism, Confirmation, Penance, Eucharist or the Body of our Lord in His due time, and Extreme Unction in the article or point of death, of such as yet be in their right mind and have their wits, or at the least wise design to receive it when they were in their right mind and had their wits. But the Sixth Sacrament, that is to say Holy Orders, of them that be perfect: and the Seventh, that is Matrimony, of such as be not perfect.

Ignorantia sacerdotum et infra.

Canon of John Peccham.

There be Seven Sacraments of Grace, the dispensators and ministers of which being Prelates of the Church. Of which Seven Sacraments Five ought to be received of every Christian man, that is to say Baptism, Confirmation, Penance, and Housel at time convenient, and Anoiling or Last Anointment, which ought to be ministered only unto such as (by tokens likely and apparent of great infirmity) seem to draw near to the peril of death, unto whom (if it may be) let it be given and ministered while they have

their right mind and perfect reason. And if it chance
or happen them to be troubled or diseased with frenzy, or
any other alienation of mind whatsoever it be, yet if
before the time of such alienation they were desirous and
took any thought or care for their soul's health, we
counsel *(consutimus)* that this Sacrament be faithfully
ministered unto them, for we believe and have also learned
by good proofs and experience that the receiving of the
said Sacrament of extreme Holy Unction will be profitable
and help a man be he never so frenetic, so that he be the
child of pre-destination or salvation, that he shall either
have time enough to return to his mind and recover his
wits again, or at the least shall obtain spiritual profit and
help of the soul to the increase of grace. There be also
two other Sacraments, that is to wit Orders and Matrimony of the which two the former . . . . . beseemeth
and agreeth only unto the perfect. The second only to
the unperfect ever since the first time of the New Testament and the law of Christ, and yet the same of the power
of the Sacrament we think giveth grace if it be contracted
with pure heart and mind.

TITULUS 8.

Of Priest's Sons.

CHAPTER I.   Summary.

*Forasmuch as the sons of persons of churches and
priests may not by the law enjoy ecclesiastical benefices
of their fathers by immediate succession, if they any such
benefices of their fathers have occupied or enjoyed, let
him be expelled and put from the same.*

Cum a jure.   Canon of John Peccham.

Forasmuch as it is forbidden by the law that the sons
of curates, parsons or priests shall not be made curates
or parsons in the same churches where as their fathers
immediately and next before them did minister, without
the Popes' dispensation before had on their behalf; and
forasmuch as it is manifest and well known by the same

law all such benefices to be vacant, if the contrary to this
be in fact and deed attempted, we do straitly charge
(*praecipimus*) and command that the prelates make
diligent inquisition of the church so being vacant, and
that they make no delay to ordain and determine the same
according to the law, taking better heed from henceforth
that they admit no such men to any such benefices by any
manner of title, lest that, contrary to justice and the
good order of the law, by such privy entering there might
seem to be a place of succession unto the inheritance of
Him that hanged upon the Cross.

TITULUS 9.

Of strange Clerks.

CHAPTER I.   Summary.

*Aliens or strangers or men unknown may not be
admitted to execute their order without letters of commendation or letters dimissory of their Ordinaries: without sufficient dispensation and proof before had of their
ordination, or Orders taking, and also admission thereunto by the Bishop.*

Cum quanta et infra.   Canon of Walter.

Such as be ordained or have taken Orders in Ireland,
Wales, or Scotland, shall not be admitted of any man
within our Province to execute their Orders so taken
except great necessity do require, and then also that they
be dispensed with by sufficient authority for and upon the
execution of the aforesaid Order, or else that the Orders
which they have taken be otherwise by their Ordinaries
ratified.

Provided nevertheless that in no wise they be admitted
before it be known of their lawful Ordination or admission to Orders, of their purity and cleanness of living,
and also of their learning: and further we command
(*praecipimus*) that no stranger and unknown priest,
whose ordination or admission to Orders is not well
known, to be admitted to serve any churches, there to

celebrate and execute the divine service, but by licence of the Bishop of the Diocese after that it shall be truly known of their Ordination or admission ... to Orders, by Letters Testimonial or witness of good and honest men, and that sufficient knowledge and proof be given and made.

CHAPTER II.   Summary.

No chaplain of a strange Diocese may be admitted to celebrate without the letters of his own Diocesan or some other Bishop unto such time as good opinion be said of his honest good manners and good behaviour.

Reverendissimae synodo et infra.

Canon of Thomas Arundell.

No chaplain shall be admitted to celebrate in any Diocese of our Province of Canterbury, other than in the which he was born or be admitted to Orders, except he bring with him the Letters of his Orders and letters of commendations of his Diocesan : and yet nevertheless the letters of other Bishops in whose Diocese in the meanwhile he hath continued and lived by long space. In the which said letters of commendation we will and command *(volumus et mandamus)* caution and warranties to be expressly made of the behaviour, manners and conversation of the same : and whether he be defamed of and upon any new opinions concerning the Catholic Faith, or of any hypocritical manners, or whether he be utterly clear and free from all such opinions : or else let as well him that doth otherwise celebrate as him that permitteth and suffereth such chaplain or priest so to sing,[6] be grievously and sharply punished.

TITULUS 10.

CHAPTER I.   Summary.

The office of the Archdeacon is to procure, provide and see that the Sacraments be duly kept and ministered and

*specially the Sacrament of the Altar, and the holy oil
must be kept under lock and key. Also the ornaments
of the churches ought to be visited and overseen by the
same Archdeacon, and the possessions of the churches
must be accounted and received.*

Ut Archidiaconi.   Canon of Stephen.

That the Archdeacons, according to the Apostle, seek
not the things which be their own, but which be of Jesu
Christ, let them see and provide in their Visitation that
the Canon of the Mass be truly corrected and that the
priests can well and right find and pronounce the words
of the Canon, and of baptising: and that they have true
and clear intelligence and perfect understanding on this
behalf, let them also teach the lay folk in what manner
and form they ought to baptise in case of necessity, that
they can and know at the least to do and minister the
same Baptism as aforesaid in some tongue, either English
or Latin or some other tongue. Let the Archdeacons see
and provide also diligently that, according to the form
and tenure of the General Council the Sacrament of the
Altar, the Chrism and Holy Oil be laid by and kept safe
under lock and key, deputed assigned and delivered to
trusty and faithful custody : also the Archdeacon ought
to have written in an inventory all the ornaments, gear
and things used in the churches: also the said Archdeacons should cause to be presented unto their sight and
to be shewed unto them all the clothes and books of the
said churches every year, that they may see what things
have been added and increased by the diligence of any
persons in the mean time, or what of the same ornaments,
clothes, books and other things have been diminished, lost,
or perished in the same mean time through malice or
negligence of any persons. And the said Archdeacons
must also provide for the possessions of the churches,
that they may every year from time to time profit increase
and prosper, that the Church in no wise be defrauded of
her right.

CHAPTER II.   Summary.

The Archdeacon must see and cause the articles of examination or sentence to be promulged, and openly recited and declared and must see also that moral precepts and teaching necessary for the health of the soul be preached by them whose office and duty it is so to do.

Eisdem etiam temporibus et infra.

Canon of John Peccham.

The Archdeacon shall diligently enquire whether the publication of the articles be made, by the which a man runneth into the sentence of excommunication in the deed doing: and as often as they can find that the priests have not preached and published to the people, at the time appointed, good moral instruction as of the 14 Articles of the Faith, of the Ten Commandments, of the two Precepts of the Gospel, of the Seven Works of Mercy ... of the Seven deadly sins, with their branches, of the Seven principal virtues, of the Seven Sacraments of Grace, of the sentences of excommunication, so often let them reprove and rebuke them and, chastising them with a canonical pain, compel them to satisfy for that wherein they negligently did offend.

CHAPTER III.   Summary.

The Archdeacon must provide that the ornaments of the altar be comely and seeming and the books of the churches convenient and the vestments of the priests to sing and to do the Office of the Mass. And the said vestments be at the least double or two for change.

Sint ecclesiarum rectores et infra.   Canon of Walter.

The Archdeacons shall provide *(provideant)* also that there be honest and clean linen clothes and other ornaments belonging to the Altar as behoveth. And also that the church have convenient books to sing and to read, and at the least two vestments for a priest to sing Mass, with all things belonging to them. And that due honour may be given and shewed in all divine services we command also *(praecipimus etiam)* that he the which ministereth to the priest at the Altar have a surplice. . . . .

CHAPTER IV.   Summary.

The Archdeacon must take good heed and see that due reparation be done to the churches.

Archidiaconi et infra.   Canon of Walter.

We do also enjoin and command the Archdeacons and their officials that, in their Visitations of the churches to be had *(faciendis)*, they take diligent consideration to the building of the church and specially of the chancel whether perchance it lack or need any reparation : and if they find any such defaults that they set a certain time under a certain pain within which they may be repaired and made up. And they shall enquire, by themselves and by their officers, whether there be any thing to be amended in any things either of the parish in which they visit, either of any the persons. And if they find any excesses or defaults there done, they shall see that they be amended either then by and by or in the next chapter.

TITULUS 11.

Of the Office of the Archpriest.

CHAPTER I.   Summary.

Every priest, specially such as have cure of souls, ought and shall clearly and plainly expound, open and declare unto his subjects four times in the year the Articles of the Faith and precepts moral necessary to the health of the soul according to the purport, effect, form and tenure of this present chapter here following.

Ignorantia sacerdotum et infra.

Canon of John Peccham.

We charge and command *(praecipimus)* that every priest bearing rule over the people plainly in their vulgar tongue without any fantastical imagination or invention of any manner sublety or curiousity either by himself or by some other, four times in the year, that is to wit every quarter of the year once, and that in one solemn feast or more the 14 Articles of the Faith, the 10 Commandments, the Two Precepts of the Gospel (that is to say of both Charities, one towards God, the other towards our neighbour), the Seven works of mercy, the Seven Deadly Sins with their branches, the Seven principal Virtues and the Seven Sacraments of Grace.

And that no man may excuse himself by ignorance in the premises, passing over the 14 Articles of the Faith afore sufficiently expounded in a title and chapter convenient going before in this present treatise, we here will touch and reckon up briefly all other things necessary to be shewed besides the said 14 Articles of the Faith as followeth,

For of the Ten Commandments of the Old Testament three precepts concern and have respect to God, and these be called the Commandments of the First Table : and seven be ordained and have respect to our neighbour, and they be called the Commandments of the Second Table.

In the First is forbidden all idolatry, when it is said, Thou shalt not have strange gods before Me. In which including be forbidden all soothsaying, all incantations and kinds of witching, with all the superstition of signs and figures and such other figments and vain inventions.

In the Second Commandment when it is said, Thou shalt not take the Name of thy God in vain, is prohibited and forbidden principally all heresy and secondly all blaspheming and unreverent naming of God and specially in perjury.

In the Third Commandment, when it is said, Remember that thou keep holy the Sabbath, is commanded the due observing of that Christian religion, to the which both clerks and lay people indifferently and equally be bound, where is to be known that the obligation or binding to keep holy day in the Sabbath legal according to the form and manner of the Old Testament is expired utterly with all the other ceremonies in the same law. And in the New Testament the manner of holy day keeping in the service of God, on the Sundays and other

solemn feasts deputed and assigned for the same by the
authority of the Church, is sufficient. In which days the
manner of keeping holy days is not to be taken of the
superstition of the Jews, but of the canonical institution
and ordinances.

The First Commandment of the Second Table is, To
honour our father and mother temporally and spiritually,
plainly expressed. And also in the same secondarily is to
be understood that every man for the merit of his degree
ought to be honoured. And in this commandment is
understood not only the father and mother carnal and
temporal, but also spiritual. So that the spiritual father
is the prelate of the Church mediate or immediate, and
the spiritual mother is the Church whose sons be all and
every Catholic person and persons.

The Second is, Thou shalt not kill, wherein is by
express words forbidden the unlawful killing or doing to
death of any person by consent, word, deed or favour :
and included in the meaning of the same—all unjust
lesion or hurting of any person is forbidden, for they
spiritually do slay and kill which do not refresh the needy,
and similarly they kill that backbite or say evil of any
person or which oppress, bear down, confound and undo
innocents or such as be faultless.

The Third Commandment is, Thou shalt do no lechery
wherein is expressedly forbidden adultery and in the meaning of the same is fornication included which is by express words prohibited and forbidden in the Deuteronomy,
where it is said, There shall be no harlots among the
daughters of Israel nor fornicator of the sons of Israel.
Also in the same commandment is forbidden all commixtion of man and woman which commixtion the good
points of matrimony, that is to say, faith, getting of
children and other offices of matrimony, do not excuse.
And also all and every voluntary or wilful pollution by
whatsoever means studiously or wilfully or willingly
procured.

The Fourth Commandment is, Thou shalt do no theft,

wherein is expressly forbidden privy contraction or handling of another man's goods against the will of the owner, and included in the meaning of the same all wrongful usurpation of another man's goods, either by fraud or guile or by usury or by violence or by fear.

The Fifth Commandment is, Thou shalt not speak against thy brother or neighbour any false witness wherein expressly is forbidden false testifying or witness bearing unto hurt, and included in the meaning of the same false testification or witness bearing for to promote any person contrary to his defects or merits. In this commandment also is condemned all manner lying, but specially pernicious and malicious.

The Sixth Commandment is, Thou shalt not desire the house of thy neighbour, which is to be understood and taken to his wrong and injury. In which is forbidden the desire of the movable possession of any man whatsoever he be and specially of any Catholic person.

The Seventh Commandment is, Thou shalt not desire the wife of thy neighbour, neither the servant nor the maid nor the ox nor the ass nor any other things that be his. In which all manner covetous desire of another man's possession as touching and concerning goods movable is prohibited and forbidden.

Now unto these Ten Commandments the Gospel further addeth Twain, that is to say the Loving of God and of our neighbour. He loveth God that keepeth the commandments above mentioned for love and not for fear or pain. And every man ought to love his neighbour as himself. In which saying this word, As himself, doth not speak nor mean equality, that every man ought to love his neighbour so much as himself in all things, but it meaneth a certain conformity, that is to say thou oughtest to love thy neighbour unto what thing thou lovest thyself that is unto good and not unto evil. And after what manner thou lovest thyself, that is spiritually and not carnally, taking carnally for viciously. Also how much thou lovest thyself, that is in prosperity and adversity, in

health and sickness.   Likewise how much thou lovest
thyself in respect of temporal things, for so much as thou
must love all men and every man above temporal riches.
Also as thyself, for so much as thou must love the soul of
thy next or his eternal soul's health more than thine own
temporal life, even likewise as thou must set more by the
life of thy soul than the life of thy flesh.   Also in what
manner thou lovest thyself, that is thou must help all men
in their necessity, as thou wouldest them to help thee in
thine.   For all these be understood in this saying, Thou
shalt love thy neighbour &c.

There be moreover six Works of Mercy opened by the
Gospel of Saint Matthew which are to Feed the hungry,
to Give drink to the thirsty, to Receive strangers to hospitality, to Clothe the naked, to Visit the sick and to Comfort the prisoners.   The seventh is taken of the Thobie[7]
which is to bury the dead.   The Seven Deadly Sins be
Pride, Envy, Wrath and Hatred, Sloth, Covetousness,
Gluttony and Lechery *(luxuria)*.

Pride is the love of his own advancement, out of which
riseth craking,[8] boasting, hypocrisy, schisms and like
other.

Envy is the hatred of another's felicity whence riseth
backbitings, slandering, grudging, strife, evil judgments
and such like.

Wrath is the desire of vengeance and of another's
harm, which after long continuance in the heart is made
hatred : this wrath is the well-spring of hurtful words
and deeds, of wounds murder and other like.

Sloth is the weariness of spiritual goodness through
which a man delighteth not in God or His laud and
honour : and is accompanied with sluggishness, cowardli-
ness, desperation and the like.

Covetousness is the immoderate love of goods movable and immovable, through unlawful getting and
keeping, from thence cometh deceit, theft, sacrilege,
simony and all filthy lucre.

Gluttony is the immoderate love of delectation in the

tasting of meat and drink, in which a man may offend
five manner of ways, that is in Time, when he eateth too
soon, too late or too oft; in Quality, when meats very
delicate be prepared; in Quantity, when too much is
eaten or drunken which is the vilest kind of gluttony.
(There is too much taken of meat or drink when it
maketh the body heavy or when it stoppeth the inward or
outward sense or when it hurteth the bodily health.) Men
also offend in greediness or hastiness of eating: and last
of all in curious dressing of their meat, to promote the
appetite withal.

As for Lechery, we may not disclose whose only fame
infecteth the whole air.

The Seven principal Virtues be Faith, Hope, Charity,
which be toward God and therefore be called theological,
Prudence, Temperance, Justice and Boldness, by these
man is ordered towards himself and his next or neighbour.

The act of Prudence is, to choose that is good: the act
of Justice is, to do right: the act of Temperance is, not
to be overcome or let with pleasures: the act of Fortitude
or Boldness is, in no wise to cease from the goodness
which is intended to be done, be it never so hard or
grievous. And these be called the four Cardinal Virtues,
that is, the four principal, for under these four be many
more of which we speak not at this time because we labour
now for the simple people.

Of the seven Sacraments of Grace we have spoken
before in their place.

CHAPTER II.   Summary.

*The priests must admonish the women of their cure
with child to have water in time of their travail ready for
Baptism in case necessity require, and also to be confessed
in time.*

Item commoneant.   Canon of Edmund.

Also the priests shall warn the women with child of
their parishes that, when they understand the time of

their travail to be at hand, they have water ready prepared to baptize the child if necessity so shall require :
and that for the great peril at hand they be confessed to
the priest, lest they be suddenly taken and may not have
him when they would.

Chapter III.   Summary.

*The priests must diligently teach their parishioners the
Word of God, lest they be counted dumb dogs, and must
quickly and speedily visit the sick.*

Presbiterorum et infra.   Canon of Stephen.

By determination of this present Council we straitly
enjoin *(duximus injungendum)* and command that persons and vicars diligently go about to inform and feed the
people committed to them, with the Word of God according to the gift given them, lest they be worthily judged
dumb dogs because with their wholesome barking they
drive not the spiritual devouring wolf from the Lord's
fold : moreover, having this saying of the Gospel in their
minds, how in the last examination the visitors of the sick
shall receive an eternal reward, as often as they shall be
sent for let them go to the sick quickly and gladly.

TITULUS 12.

Of the Office of a Vicar.

Chapter I.   Summary.

*None shall be admitted to a vicarage but he that pur-
poseth to be present and to be priested at the next Orders,
he that is otherwise admitted shall be repelled.*

Cum hostis et infra.   Canon of the same Stephen.

We decree that no Bishop of our Province shall admit
to a Vicarage any person except he will personally minister in the church where the vicarage is given him and
except he be such as within short time may be made priest.

And if any be admitted and will not be priested, he
shall lose the benefice.

Chapter II.

Quoniam autem et infra.   The same Stephen.

We ordain *(statuimus)* that unto a perpetual vicar the fruits of 5 marks[9] at the least be assigned which was wont to be let to farm for 5 marks, those parts of Wales excepted, in which perchance through the smallness of the churches the vicars can be content with less stipend. The Diocesan shall also consider the power of the church and see whether the vicar shall bear the charges of the person or both together, so that the Archdeacon, where he shall receive proxy of both or of one of them, shall be contented with one proxy only.

TITULUS 13.

Of the Office of a Judge being Ordinary.

Chapter I.

Statuimus auctoritate.   Canon of Stephen.

We ordain and decree *(statuimus)* by the authority of this present Council, that all and every prelate have to their almoners men of honesty. And that the prelates themselves according to the Apostle keep hospitality and be men of alms, and that at hours convenient they personally come where they may be seen abroad, as well for to hear the poor as also to exhibit and minister justice : and that in their own persons they be sometimes present at the hearing of confessions and enjoining of penance.

Chapter II.

Item statuimus.   Canon of Boniface.

We also decree *(statuimus)* that Bishops in their Synods and other convocations, and all Archdeacons in their chapters and ministers of parish churches in their churches, shall three times in the year denounce unto all that will enjoy the privilege of a clerk that they wear openly and in due place the competent weed *(habitum)* and tonsure of a clerk and specially before their Ordinaries and in churches and congregations of clerks.

TITULUS 14.

Of Superiority and Obedience.

Presbiteri et infra.   Canon of Robert Winchelsey.

It must be enjoined *(debet injungi)* under the virtue of obedience to all chaplains that be admitted to sing in any church within our Province, that they be present on the Sundays and other Holy Days when and where Matins, Mass and other hours be said by note, to sing and read : upon the which things we will that an oath be taken of them and given at their admission. Also we will bind the priests by the same oath that they shall take nothing away from the persons, vicars and presidents[10] of the churches or chapels whereas they sing, but shall humbly obey them and give due reverence.

TITULUS 15.

Of Truce and Peace.

Magna nobis et infra.   Canon of Edmund.

We do straitly command *(praecipimus)* that the persons and vicars and other curates of the churches have peace with all men (as much as in them is) and that they monish their parishioners to be, through the unity of faith and the bond of peace, one body in Christ. And that they cease diligently and make quiet the displeasures if any spring in their parishes, calling them in amity and concord that be at variance, not suffering (as much as in them lieth) the sun to go down upon the anger of their parishioners.

TITULUS 16.

Of Transactions.

Caeterum districtius.   Canon of Stephen.

Furthermore we thought straitly to be commanded *(duximus inhibendum)* that no Archdeacons and their officials or other judges for the prosperity or good continuance of peace, if they that were at variance will agree together, may ask or require anything; but that it shall be lawful, for the parties asking licence, to depart by composition from the law when they will, so that the matter be such as may admit composition; nor shall punish either the plaintiff or defendant without open knowledge of their unrighteousness.

TITULUS 17.
Of Pleading.

Chapter I.

Quoniam per advocatos.   Canon of Stephen.

Because that by advocates often times matrimonies be disturbed, we ordain, that whereas a sentence is given for matrimony, the advocate which standeth against the same shall in that deed doing be deprived of his advocation, for a year without the judge have him excused, by express words in the same sentence, for just error or probable ignorance.

Chapter II.

Veloces ad audiendum et infra.
                              Canon of John Peccham.

No man from henceforth shall be admitted to exercise openly the office of advocation without he have first heard the Canon Law and Civil Law at the least three years with good diligence. And the surety thereof shall he make good by his own oath whereas it doth not appear by condign testimony nor by deed.

TITULUS 18.
Of Procurations.

Exhorrenda et infra.   Canon of John Peccham.

We decree *(statuimus)* that no Dean nor Archdeacon or his official or official of Bishop shall put his seal to any proxy, or to any commandment in which power is

F

granted to any procurator,[11] without it be asked of him openly in the Court, or else out of the Court, whereas he which hath constituted the procurator and is plainly known to be the true master is present corporally requiring the same, so that all manner of deceit may be excluded and let apart. And whatsoever Dean, Archdeacon or his official or official of the Bishops of evil mind do the contrary for three years, he shall be suspended from office and benefice. Whatsoever procurator also do procure feigned or false proxy to be made shall be suspended for three years from his office of proctorship, and shall be unable to obtain any benefice of the Church, and, if he be married or be a bigamist, he shall be under excommunication in that deed doing. And that which is done or procured by such a feigned or false procurator shall be utterly reputed as no deed. And the procurator also himself which is the worker of all the falsehood shall be exempted for ever from all lawful acts. And all this persons nevertheless if they may be convict upon the same shall be bound to restore to the party damaged all his interest and loss.

Thus endeth the First Book.

THE SECOND BOOK.

TITULUS 1.

Of Judgments.

CHAPTER I.

In causis et infra.   Canon of Stephen.

We decree *(statuimus)* that deans rural from henceforth shall not presume to hear any cause of matrimony, but that the examination of them shall be committed only to discreet men, in whose presence if it may conveniently be done the sentence shall be afterward given.

CHAPTER II.

Quidam Ruralium et infra.   Canon of John Peccham.

We ordain *(statuimus)* that no certificate signed under the seal of any dean rural shall be given to any person, or shall at any time be granted, without that it upon some solemn day be first openly recited in the church at Masstime whereas he that is cited doth dwell or is most conversant: this mean and order being thereto adjoined, that he which is cited may have sufficient leisure and time that he may conveniently appear at the day and place to him preferred : but if so be that in any case the time do so constrain that there be no manner of delay to be had, then the citation being openly done before witnesses, the certificate shall be given in the church or in an open place before faithful and substantial witnesses, so that the day of citation and place be expressed in the same certificate. And so shall the certificate in no wise be made before the citation be executed and done : and let the deans rural swear every year in the Bishop's Synod that they shall faithfully do the same.

CHAPTER III.

Item omnes illi et infra.   Canon of Simon Mepham.

That the violators and disturbers of the immunity and liberties of the church, that is to say that such secular persons as at any time hereafter shall presume to withdraw, take away, consume, waste or handle any manner thing out of the houses, manors, granges or other places to the Archbishops, Bishops, or to any other ecclesiastical persons or to the Church's self appertaining and belonging, against the will and without the permission and sufferance of the lords or of them that be deputed and assigned keepers of such things, or that cause anything as aforesaid to be withdrawn, taken away, wasted, consumed or handled or shall ratify, uphold or maintain any such withdrawing, taking away, consuming, wasting or handling in any manner as aforesaid done in their names or by any of their familiars, may not eschew nor avoid through the occasion of hardness and difficulty in acciting of them, as often times heretofore it hath happened, but that due process may be had and made against them as there ought to be. By the consent and assent of all our brethren and of all this convocation, we decree and ordain *(decrevimus)* that every such violator as aforesaid whatsoever he be, if he may personally be found or may be safely and surely be come unto, shall be called to appear personally. And if he cannot be found or cannot be surely and safely come unto, then the same violator as aforesaid shall be cited at his own house (if he have any house) where he may surely be cited and safely. But if he can not be surely and safely cited at his own house, then we decree and ordain a citation to be made in the Parish Church of his dwelling house or if he have none or be not known that he hath any such dwelling that then the citation be had and made in the Cathedral Church of that place in which the said immunity and liberty of the church is said and reported to be violated, disturbed and hurted. And nevertheless also in the Parish Church of the same place we decree citation to be made, if it may be

surely done and without peril, willing and also ordaining
and decreeing that by virtue and force of every such
citation at the house or churches openly made as aforesaid, not only in the cases above written, but also in all
cases of the constitution and ordinance of Otho Bonus,
late legate of the See Apostolic in England, which
beginneth in Latin—*Ad tutelam* (in English, *For the
safeguard and defence*).

As hereafter in the end of this work ensueth, the party
so cited to be constrained and forced as though he had
been personally apprehended and taken by the same citation, and that by virtue of the same citation process may
be made against the party so cited with all such effect as
might have been if the said party had been personally
cited. And further we ordain and decree *(decernimus)*
that all the foresaid and also all other violators and disturbers of the liberty and immunity of the Church whatsoever they be, may be convented in the place where such
trespass or offence shall be done, although they can not
there be found, as well by the officer of the judge as also
at the instance of the party. And whether such violators
and disturbers of the immunities and liberties of the
Church as aforesaid can be found or surely and safely
come to or gotten or not, and whether they have a house
or not, we will and decree *(volumus)* that it remain in
doubt of the certificate of him unto the which the citation
is committed and commanded to be made. And that such
as have suffered any injury or wrong in the cases above
mentioned may the lightlier obtain due justice by probation of this Provincial Council we straitly command
(praecipimus) that all ordinary judges of our Province
of Canterbury help one another, without any difficulty in
speeding of citations and executions of the same and all
other lawful commandments.

CHAPTER IV.

Excussis et infra.   Canon of John Stratford.

Because that Bishops and Archdeacons and their
officials and other ordinaries and their commissaries do

command oftentimes original citations concerning the
corrections of transgressors to be executed by the persons,
vicars, or their parish priests, it is therefore laid to their
charges that they do craftily disclose their confessions that
be cited, made to them privily in the court of their souls
of and upon such things as they be cited for, wherefore
parishioners be grievously offended and thenceforth do
refuse to confess their sins unto them, we do decree
(statuimus) that such primary citations as shall be made
by the authority of the said ordinaries be not hereafter
commanded to be done by the said persons and other, but
let them be executed by the officials, deans, summoners or
other their officers.   And if such primary citations be
directed to persons, vicars, or priests they shall not be
bound to obey in that behalf.   But the said primary citations and judgments and processes that follow out of
the same shall be void and of none effect by the law.

TITULUS 2.

Of a Court Competent.

CHAPTER I.

Contingit aliquando.   Canon of Boniface.

It happeneth sometimes that the clerks although they
be not taken in the deed doing or convicted as evildoers
or suspect of crime or trespass or wrongdoing to any man,
be nevertheless taken by the lay power[12] without any
regard of persons, and be cast into prison, and be not
delivered to their ordinaries when they do require them
to be freely judged after the Canon Laws.   And if the
clerks to whom crimes be laid do not appear before the
secular judges when they be called they be banished out
of the realm.

And because in this the liberty of the Church is confounded and broken when a clerk is judged by a lay judge,
we do decree that, if the clerks that so be taken be known
and be honest, as well the takers as the withholders of

them and they that refuse to deliver them at the ordinary's request shall be openly declared excommunicate by the ordinaries of the places where they dwell. And the places also where they be detained and the lands of the takers and detainers of them shall be under the Church interdiction until such time as they be delivered to their ordinaries and convenient satisfaction and amends be made for such excesses. And they which laid to their charges such false crimes or maliciously did feign lies or deceits for the which they were taken and wrongfully detained shall be likewise declared excommunicate seeing they be excommunicated by the authority of the Council of Oxford in the deed doing. But if the clerks, which be taken and detained be wanderers and unknown, if they be found in the possession of clerkship they shall be required by the ordinaries of the places of the king or of him that hath power to deliver them, that he will deliver them freely to be judged by the Church.

And if they be denied, process shall be made against the resisters and detainers by the penalties above rehearsed : but if the clerks restored to the churches be amerced by the secular judge for any personal transgression the prelates shall not compel the said clerks to pay the same amerciaments seeing they were not condemned of their own judges. And if it chance the prelates to be distrained or attached for the same they shall defend themselves against such attachments or distresses by the foresaid remedies. The same thing shall be done as often as men of the Church be amerced by a secular judge for any such things as are known merely to appertain to the spiritual court.

Chapter II.

Certain things taken out of the King's Answers.
Circumspecte agatis et infra.

Canon of John Stratford.

As concerning the matter and business which is touching to the Bishop of Norwich and his clergy, not to

punish them if they hold play for those things that be
mere spiritual, as for corrections which the prelates exercise for deadly sin, as for fornication, adultery and such
other, for the which sometimes corporal punishment,
sometimes pecuniary is enjoined, specially if he that is
convict be a gentleman *(liber homo):* also if the prelate
punish for that the Church is not made or the churchyard
not closed, or the Church not covered, or not comely
ornated, in which cases no other pain can be set but
pecuniary : also if a person ask of his parishioners oblations or tithes due or accustomed, or if one person plead
against another person for tithes great or small, so long
as the fourth part of the Church's goods be not asked :
also if the person ask a mortuary in these parties where
mortuaries are used to be given : also if the prelate or
advocate *(i.e. patron)* of any church ask of the person
any pension due to him, for all such pensions ought to be
asked in the spiritual court : also for laying violent hands
on a priest and in cause of defamation, plea shall be kept
in the spiritual court, so long as it is done for the correction of sin and no money is asked or required.

CHAPTER III.   Summary.

*Whatsoever clerks or lay do craftily or maliciously
proceed by the King's briefs against them that be faultless
and unknowing and as many as favour them that so do
proceed shall suffer the sentence of the great excommunication.*

Dierum invalescens malicia et infra.

Canon of John Stratford.

Insomuch as certain of our Province, maliciously intending against other, do craftily and privily obtain the
King's briefs, or accounts, or trespass, or other writs
against them whom they intend to hurt, to be directed
into strange counties where their adversaries never were
nor made contract or fault, nor ministered the goods of
any other, and by that means so privily prosecuteth, their

adversaries knowing nothing thereof, that they be other outlawed or banished the realm wherefore, seeing that all process and sentence made, against them that be thus unknowing and undefended, is justly by the law reproved. And that the malice of man ought not to be spared or favoured, we ordain *(statuimus)* that whosoever of our Province, whether they be clerks or lay, that hereafter privily, craftily, or maliciously (as beforesaid) do obtain and prosecute, make and procure briefs, or wittingly give counsel, help, or favour unto the same, or ratifieth and uphold them made in his name shall in the deed doing fall into the sentence of the great curse.

Chapter IV.   Summary.

All that have ordinary jurisdiction must keep their consistories, sessions and chapters in places notable and meet for victual or else they shall be suspended from church entry.

Excussis et infra.   Canon of John Stratford.

We do consider and plainly perceive that, by means that certain officials of Bishops, Archdeacons and other Ordinaries of our Province which keep their consistories, sessions and chapters yearly from three weeks to three, or from four to four, in divers places of their jurisdictions and deaneries, do often times decline in those places where sale victual is hard to be gotten, and charge with excessive costs the persons and vicars of such places as they keep their consistories, sessions and chapters in, or of like places nigh hand to their great slander and reproof, for, if the persons and vicars of the Churches at such times do not costly receive the officials after their desire, they seek colours and feign causes by the which they grievously molest and vex them. For the which things and other unjust causes, by determination of this present Council, we ordain *(statuimus)* that all such consistories, sessions and chapters from henceforth be kept in places most notable of the said jurisdictions and deaneries, or at the least where victuals may commonly be found to sale. And that the officials and every ministers of ordinaries do their offices at their masters' costs, as well in keeping such consistories, sessions and chapters as in other acts which they exercise for their masters; and as for citations made unto such consistories, sessions and chapters that be appointed to be kept in other places than is above mentioned with all process as shall happen hereafter to be made in them, we declare to be none effect by the Law.

And if the said officials, if they for the speeding of their masters' business require or execute costs of the said subjects, or do vex or trouble them through occasion of non-payment of such expenses, we will *(volumus)* to remain suspended in so doing from their office and church entry.

TITULUS 3.

Of Holy Days.

CHAPTER I.   Summary.

Good Friday which is Holy must be spent wholly in holy and godly service.

Animarum saluti prospicere cupientes.

Canon of Simon Mepham.

According to our mind and desire, which moveth us to look unto the health of man's soul, we make our beginning at the very fountains of the Saviour. And therefore we establish *(statuimus et ordinamus)* and ordain that Holy Friday, in the which our Saviour the Lord Jesus Christ after He had suffered many beatings and wounds gave up His precious soul upon the Cross, shall be kept solemnly after the manner and custom of the Church in reading with silence, in praying with fasting, in compunction, that is in wailing of sins with tears. By the authority also of this present Council we straitly forbid *(inhibemus)* that no person henceforth intend upon that day vile works, or exercise any other than works of mercy; notwithstanding we make no law unto the poor men hereby, neither yet do we forbid the rich men to minister in the way of charity their accustomed help whereby the poor man's tillage is furthered.

Chapter II.   Summary.

The Feast of the Conceiving of the Holy Virgin Mary shall be kept holily and solemnly.

Ad haec quia inter omnes sanctos.

Canon of Simon Mepham.

Furthermore because among all saints the memory of the Most Blessed Virgin Mary, Mother of the Lord, is kept both often and solemn, and that so much the more as she is thought to have found greater favour with God, Who hath certainly ordained her conception, predestinated unto the temporal birth and Incarnation of His Only Begotten and unto the health of all people, that by this means the first beginning of our health (though they be somewhat far off) may increase devotion and health in all people, which have in their devout hearts spiritual joys, we ordain and straitly *(statuimus et firmiter praecipiendo mandamus)* command that the Feast of the said Conception be holily and solemnly from henceforth kept in all churches of our Province of Canterbury, which thing we do following the steps of venerable Anselm our predecessor, who considering other elder feasts of the said Virgin thought the Feast of her Conception worthy to be added.

Chapter III.   Summary.

The Feasts contained in this law must be kept solemnly in all other a man may do his accustomed work unpunished.

Ex Scripturis et infra.   Canon of Simon Islepe.

By advisement and counsel of our brethren we be appointed *(duximus)* to recite in these presents the holy

days in which men must abstain generally throughout
our Province of Canterbury from all servile labours (yea
though they be such as be profitable to the common weal).
First the holy Sunday, which shall begin at the evening
hour of the Saturday, and not before that hour, lest we
should seem to be partakers of the Jew's profession which
thing shall also be observed in all feasts that have their
vigils. The Feast also of the Lord's Nativity, of Saint
Stephen, John Evangelist, Innocents, Thomas the Martyr,
the Circumcision of our Lord, Epiphany of the Lord, the
Purification of the Blessed Virgin Mary, the Feast of
Saint Matthias the Apostle, the Annunciation of the
Blessed Mary, the Feast of Pasche with three days following, Saint Mark the Evangelist, the Feast of the
Apostles Philip and Jacob, the Invention of the Holy
Cross, the Ascension of our Lord, Pentecost with three
days following, the Feast of Christ's Body, the Nativity
of John Baptist, the Feast of the Apostles Peter and Paul,
the Translation of Saint Thomas, the Feasts of Saint
Mary Magdalene, of Saint James the Apostle, of Saint
Laurence, of the Assumption of the Blessed Mary, of
Saint Bartholomew, of the Nativity of the Blessed Mary,
of the Exaltation of the Holy Cross, of Saint Matthew
the Apostle and Evangelist, of Saint Michael, of Saint
Luke Evangelist, of the Apostles Simon and Jude, of All
Saints, of Saint Andrew the Apostle, of Saint Nicholas,
of the Conception of the Blessed Mary, of Saint Thomas
the Apostle, the solemnities of the dedications of parish
churches and of the saints in whose honour the parish
churches be dedicate, and other Feasts which for certain
causes are specially commanded in every diocese of the
said Province by the Ordinaries of the places, & infra.
In all other Feasts of Saints the used and accustomed
works may be done without punishment.

CHAPTER IV.   Summary.

The Feast of Saint George the Martyr shall be kept
double after the manner of the more double feast, as well
by the clergy as the lay, the Feasts also of the holy
Bishops David and Chad and likewise of Winefrede the
Virgin shall be celebrate in their days with " regimine
chori " and nine lessons.

Ineffabilis et infra.   Canon of Henry Chicheley.

We that desire the laud of God to be enlarged and
amplified in His Saints, in the which He is glorified, in
our Province be moved hereunto, as well by the King's
exhortations and the inhabitants of this realm as by the
counsels of our fellow brethren and clergy of our Province, yea and also be assisted with the conformation and
decree of our Provincial Council. And therefore following the godly and devout mind and affection of the old
Fathers towards the Saints of God, by the express consent
of our brethren the clergy aforesaid we will ordain and
command *(volumus statuimus et praecipimus)* the Feast
of the Blessed Martyr S. George to be kept solemn, under
double office and after the manner of the more double
feast, every year in all times to come, as well by the clergy
as the people of the said Province throughout all churches
of the same : and we command *(praecipimus)* all to cease
upon that Feast from all servile works through all cities
and places of the same Province, even likewise as they do
upon Christmas Day, that the faithful people may the
rather upon that day come together unto their churches to
the laud, and praise of God, and may the more devoutly
call for the help of that Saint, and the oftener pray for
the King and the wealth of the realm, moreover by the
authority of the said Provincial Council we ordain
(decernimus) and also establish *(statuimus)* by these
presents that the Feasts of SS. David and Chadd Bishops
and of Wenefrede the Virgin from henceforth throughout all our Province be kept in their times assigned, that
is the Feast of S. David the first day, of Saint Chad the

second day of March, of Wenefrede the third day of
November with *regimine chori* & nine lessons in all times
to come.

CHAPTER V.   Summary.

*The Feast of the putting down of Saint John of
Beaverley, Confessor and Bishop, shall be kept the
seventh day of May as the feast of one Confessor and
Bishop of Easter time " cum regimine chori " after the
custom of Sarum, but the day of his translation shall be
kept with the Feast of Crispin and Crispinian.*

Anglicanae ecclesiae et infra.

Canon of Henry Chicheley.

By the wills and assents of our brethren our clergy
being present in this Council, and nevertheless at the
special instance and request of our King the most
christened prince, we have minded *(duximus exaltandam)*
the memory of the most blessed Confessor and Bishop,
John Beverlack, to be enhanced everywhere throughout
our Province with devout minds and vows. And therefore we establish and, by the counsel and assent of our
foresaid brethren, we ordain for all times hereafter to
come that the Feast of the deposition of the said saint
which is known to fall the seventh day of May, that is in
the Morrow of Saint John before the Latin gate, be per-
petually kept throughout our said Province after the
manner of one Confessor and Bishop of Easter season
" cum regimine chori " after the use of Sarum,[13] but for
so much as in the Feast of his translation, which falleth
yearly the twenty-fifth day of October, it hath been of
old time accustomed in all churches almost of the said
Province to serve the Saints Crispin and Crispinian after
the use of Sarum. Therefore lest the bringing in of one
feast should be the excluding of another, but rather that
under the gladness of one feast the said Martyrs might
be honoured together with the said noble Confessor, by
the agreeable consent of our said brethren and the clergy
we establish, decree and ordain *(statuimus decernimus et*

ordinamus) that henceforth yearly the said twenty-fifth
day of October shall be celebrate everywhere through our
Province with nine lessons, whereof three first shall be
proper to Saint Crispin and Crispinian, and three mean of
a Translation of Saint John before named, and three last
of the exposition of the gospel of many martyrs with the
service that is used in like feasts after Sarum.

TITULUS 4.

Of sequestring possession and fruits.

ONE CHAPTER.   Summary.

*Violators of sequestrations made in cases by the law
permitted after publication made in due time and place
shall incur the sentence of the great excommunication,
except there be a lawful appeal from the same sequestration.*

Frequens perversorum et infra.

Canon of John Stratford.

By deliberation of this present council we establish
(statuimus) that whosoever within our Province do
violate or break sequestrations, made by the Bishops or
their Vicars general or their Officials principal for just
causes and true and by the law permitted, in the church
goods, or in other after publications be once duly made
in such places as the sequestered goods be, shall incur in
so doing the sentence of the great excommunication:
nevertheless if appellation be made from the sequestration
and be lawfully prosecuted, hanging the appeal, the possessioners of the sequestered goods and other may use
the same goods freely and unpunished.

TITULUS 5.

Of Presumptions.

ONE CHAPTER.   Summary.

*None that renounceth or giveth up his church may re-
ceive of his substitute the vicarage of the same if he do*

both shall be deprived, this of his vicarage and he of his personage.

Ne lepra et infra.   Canon of Stephen.

We forbid *(inhibemus)* any manner person renouncing or giving up his church to receive of his substitute the vicarage of the same, inasmuch as it may be vehemently suspected or presumed that such things be done by unlawful pactions, but if any presume to do it the one shall be deprived from his vicarage and the other from his personage.

TITULUS 6.

Of Oaths.

CHAPTER I.

Presenti statuto definimus.   Canon of Stephen.

We determine *(definimus)* by this present statute that the Bishop shall receive an oath of him that is presented, that he hath neither promised neither given ought for that presentation unto the presenter, neither made any compaction with him for it, specially if he that is presented seem likely to be suspected thereof.

CHAPTER II.

Evenit et infra.   Canon of Boniface the Archdeacon.

We establish *(statuimus)* that, when the prelates and ecclesiastical judges inquire the faults and excesses of their subjects that deserve punishment, the lay be compelled if need require by sentences of excommunication to give an oath to say the truth; and if any withstand or let this oath to be given, he shall be bridled with the sentence of excommunication and interdiction.

CHAPTER III.   Summary.

Stipendiary Chaplains that will serve in a parish church before they celebrate must give an oath to keep fidelity toward their superiors and peace and concord amongst all the parishioners as much as in them is, if any be convict of perjury he shall be forbidden his office but these oaths ought gently to be received of their superiors.

Presbiteri stipendiarii et infra.

Canon of Robert Winchelsea.

The said priests shall swear the Sunday or Holy day after their admission at Mass time, before the persons vicars or such as be in their stead or else before the ordinaries of that place, the Holy Scriptures opened before them and looked upon, that they shall work no harm or prejudice to the parish churches or chapels in which they celebrate, or unto the persons or vicars, or unto them that keep their places or have any manner of interest about their offerings, portions, fruits, mass pence, minds trentals, or any other manner rights what name soever they bear, but rather, as much as in them is, shall keep and save them harmless in the premises.

The said priests shall also specially swear that they shall in no wise raise uphold or nourish hatred, evil occasions, tidings and strifes betwixt the person and the parishioners, but as much as in them is shall nourish and keep concord amongst them. We will moreover and firmly enjoining command *(volumus insuper et firmiter injungendo mandamus)* that the priests above named presume not to celebrate in such churches and chapels before they have given an oath under the form aforesaid, if so be the persons or vicars or other above specified will and require them so to be sworn, decreeing and ordaining that, if any such priest presume to celebrate contrary to this prohibition in any place so forbade, in so doing shall incur irregularity beside other pains which the Canons doth appoint to the violators of holy constitutions, but if it chance the said chaplains (being as aforesaid sworn) to be convicted by lawful proofs before a competent judge upon the violation of such their oath, or thereof be defamed and can not make their purgation, they shall be utterly removed and forbidden as perjured persons to

G

celebrate within our Province until such season as they
shall be dispensed with canonically therein and infra : and
the said persons or vicars, or such as keep their places,
ought gently receive the said oaths and shall have a copy
in their churches of the premises and other statutes that
be made in this behalf.

TITULUS 7.

Of Appeals.

CHAPTER I.

Frequens perversorum et infra.

Canon of John Stratford.

If appellation be made from the sequestration and be
lawfully prosecuted as long as the appeal hangeth the
possessioner of the sequestered goods and other may use
them freely without punishment.

CHAPTER II.

In Concilio Oxoniensi.   Canon of Simon Mepham.

In a Council kept at Oxford a certain statute[14] was
made (as it is said), by the which, amongst other things
men be forbid frivolly to appeal from any judicial grief
before the definite sentence; and that all advocates and
procurators of that consistory shall be bound by an oath
and by other things in the statute contained to the observation thereof, and shall be punished if they anything do to
the contrary: which statute, although it be overcast in
the outside with a fair colour of words, yet in very deed
it is brought in to take away the remedy of appeal from
them that be oppressed. And therefore we utterly reprove
and disannul that statute and whatsoever hath followed
thereof: and all them that have made any other to
observe that statute we absolve from the same.

The End of the Second Book.

THE THIRD BOOK.

TITULUS 1.
Of the life and honesty of Clerks.

CHAPTER I.   Summary.

All prelates named in this Constitution must go in Clerkly habit and close gown, neither any clerk shall go in a long busch or in a lay garment, but only in case of lawful fear and let all be compelled to avoid surfeiting and drunkenness.

Ut clericalis ordinis.

Canon of Stephen.   Act of Convocation, 1557.

That the due honour of the order of clerks may be observed and kept, we ordain, *(decernimus)* by authority of this present Council, that as well Archdeacons as Deacons and all other that be put in pre-eminence and dignity, likewise all Deans Rural and priests, shall go comely in clerkly habit and shall use close gowns : the same thing let the officials of the said Archdeacons do when they be in the Consistory : moreover none of these clerks neither any other shall nourish their hair, but must go honestly rounded and conveniently crowned, except perchance any just cause of fear shall require his habit to be transformed : let all clerks also utterly and diligently abstain from much eating and drinking and other things which deface their honesty; and to observe and keep all these things diligently they shall be straitly compelled by their superiors according to the form of the general council.

CHAPTER II.

Quamvis religionis.   Canon of John Peccham.

Cleaving fast to the statute of Lord Othobone, once legate in England of the Apostolic See, we ordain and straitly command *(praecipimus)* that every clerk being in

Holy Orders wear his outward garments unlike to the garments of warriors or the lay, which be badged before and behind, or at the least unlike in fashion for the honesty that becometh them, and whosoever presume otherwise to do, as long as he beareth the habit of a contrary fashion he shall be suspended from Church entry: and whereas the legate aforesaid hath made a decree against clerks that wear coif openly before the prelates or the people, that, if they be monished and amend not in so doing, they shall be suspended from their office in which state they stand three months: they shall then be suspended from their benefice, from which suspension they shall not be absolved, but they give the sixth part of the goods of their Church to be distributed to the poor people by the Bishop's Hands, and yet shall nevertheless be otherwise punished at the arbitrament of the prelates.

We, perceiving that statute to have been hitherto of small efficacy, because that the inferior prelates dare not monish such monstrous clerks (and therefore through their cowardness some be fallen into the pains limited by the said legates) and such clerks seldom shew themselves in the Bishop's sight, do therefore decree *(statuimus)* and establish that, all monitions ceasing (seeing the ignorance of the law may not excuse clerks), as often as they wear such coifs openly before the people and prelates except it chance in journeying, for their arrogant frowardness shall fall in all the said penalties: we command moreover that hereafter special inquisition be made for such in every deanery: and, of what degree or pre-eminence soever they be, that process be made against them according to the form of the law.

Chapter III.

Exterior habitus et infra.   Canon of John Stratford.

By approbation of this holy council we establish and command *(praecipimus)* that whosoever obtain ecclesiastical benefices in our province (specially such as be

within holy orders) bear the habit and tonsure of clerks
competent unto their state. And if any clerks of our
province go openly within the same, having their superior
vesture notable short or strait, or their sleeves exceeding
long and large hanging down so that their cubits may be
seen uncovered, or with their hair unrounded, or with
long beards, or use rings openly upon their fingers (except
such as it becometh by reason of their dignity and
honour), or else exceed in the premises or any part thereof, except when they be warned they amend themselves
and effectually, within six months after they be found
faulty, cast from them all such excesses, if they be beneficed (the six months once passed) they shall incur suspension from their office in so doing. In which suspension,
if they stand three months following, they shall be
suspended from their benefices without any monition by
the law, neither shall they be absolved from such sentence
by their diocesans (to whom we reserve their absolution
by the authority of this present council) before they have
paid the fifth part of one year's fruits of their ecclesiastical benefices, which part shall be faithfully distributed
within three months after, by the same diocesans in whose
diocese they obtain such benefices, unto such poor people
as dwell in the places of their benefices, and if they
meddle with the divine service and with the administration of the said benefices, as they did before so long as
such suspensions doth endure, in so doing shall be deprived from their benefices : but as touching clerks that
be not beneficed and shew themselves openly and commonly for clerks, if they walk at large in the premises or
any part thereof, except when they be monished they
effectually within six months amend themselves, for so
doing shall stand unable by the space of four months to
obtain ecclesiastical benefice. And besides all this, such
as bear themselves for clerks and be students at the Universities of our said province, if they with effect abstain
not from the premises shall be unable in so doing unto all
degrees and honours in those Universities, until they
shew in their manners and outward behaviour ripe dis-

cretion and sadness that becometh honest scholars : other
penalties that be made against such transgressors nevertheless standing in their effect and might. And yet will
we not forbid by this present constitution but that clerks
may use in places and times convenient their supertunicles
with competent sleeves (in which they were wont to sit
at their meat), and also when they journey may take and
use short and narrow garments, as it shall seem to them
good for the time only of their journey : but, for so much
as Bishops may not boldly rebuke other if they correct not
themselves and their own household in this behalf, we
ordain that the Bishops of our Province observe and keep
becomeliness in tonsure, garments and other things before
rehearsed, and cause the clerks of their house likewise
to do.

TITULUS 2.

Of the dwelling together of Clerks and Women.

ONE CHAPTER.

Ut clericalis ordinis et infra.   Canon of Stephen.

Clerks that have benefices or holy orders may not be
bold to keep concubines openly in their houses, neither
may have open haunt to them in any other place with
slander. And if it chance that their concubines, having
open monition, will not depart from them, let them be
even driven from the Church of God which they have
presumed so to slander, let them not be admitted nor
received unto ecclesiastical sacraments : and if they will
not so abstain, let them be stricken with the sword of excommunication, and then at last let the secular power be
called upon against them : and as for the clerks themselves, after they be once canonically monished, we will
they be looked upon by subtraction of their office and
benefice.

TITULUS 3.

Of the Clerks that be married.

CHAPTER I.

Si qui clerici. Canon of Richard.

If any clerks under the orders of sub-deacon contract matrimony in no wise may they be separated from their wives, except by their common consent they will go to religion and there continue in the service of God, but as long as they live with their wives they may by no means receive ecclesiastical benefice. And they which being in the orders of sub-deacon or above, get them unto matrimony shall leave their women, although they be never so loth and will not thereunto consent.

CHAPTER II.

Cum ex eo quod clerici. Canon of Henry Chicheley.

Because that clerks married, bigamous and also lay persons do take upon them to exercise ecclesiastical jurisdiction, and to enquire and search, punish and correct, sometime in their own name and sometime under the shadows and cloak of another man's name, such crimes and excesses as appertain to the judgment and punishment of the Church and to decree letters of excommunication and suspension; and also be scribes and registers of such matters of correction and the keepers of the same registers, by means whereof the Church suffereth no little slander and the authority and censure thereof is little regarded. Therefore we, purposing to withstand such slanders and to look upon the honesty and honour of the Church in following the steps of the holy canons, by the authority of this council ordain and establish *(ordinamus et statuimus)* that no clerk married, bigamous, or lay, shall exercise from henceforth within our province of Canterbury any manner spiritual jurisdiction, under any colour either in his own name or any other person's name, or shall be scribe or register in causes of correction, that

is to say, when process is made for the correction of the
soul or by office of the judge, or by any means shall be
the keeper of the register of such corrections : and whatsoever ordinary under the degree of a Bishop, or other
person having ecclesiastical jurisdiction do presume to
take and receive a clerk, married, lay, or bigamous, unto
the premises, or any of them, or, after the space of two
months from the time of publication of this constitution,
do wittingly suffer or keep him in the office of such jurisdiction, or do not really remove him which is admitted or
shall hereafter be admitted, he shall incur in so doing the
pain of suspension from exercising such jurisdiction and
also from Church entry : moreover whatsoever citations,
processes, sentences, acts and gestes be had or made by
the said clerks, married, lay, or bigamous, in the premises,
or any of them after the manner before rehearsed, shall
be of no value but shall be vain, void and of none effect in
the law. And the same clerks, married, bigamous, or lay,
if they take upon them the premises, or any of them,
contrary to the prohibition of this present council, shall
incur in so doing the sentence of the great excommunication.

TITULUS 4.
Of the Clerks that be not resident.
CHAPTER I.
Statuimus et infra.   Canon of Stephen.

Bishops must provide and see that they be resident in
their Cathedral Churches in some great feasts, and at the
least in some part of Lent, as it shall seem to them
expedient for the soul's health.

CHAPTER II.
Cum hostis antiquus et infra.   Canon of Stephen.

We must diligently beware that the care of the Lord's
flock be not committed unto such as either through
negligence will not, either through ignorance cannot dili-

gently intend (as it becometh) the charge committed unto them. And therefore we ordain *(statuimus)* that no Bishop admit any to a vicarage, except he will personally minister in the Church where the vicarage is that is given him : and also he be such one as may within short time be ordered into a priest, but if any be admitted and will not be a priest he shall lose his vicarage. And because it is against honesty that Churches should stand desolate of shepherds through their small advantages and profits, we ordain by this present decree that Churches which be not in profits above five marks shall not be given but to such persons as may be resident in the same and minister in their own persons, but if it chance any such to be admitted as will not be resident or minister in the same after they be once warned by the Bishop of the diocese, let them be deprived, since the Lord's bread ought not to be given but to them that labour.

CHAPTER III.

Preterea et infra. Canon of John Peccham.

We establish *(statuimus)* that persons which make not corporal residence in their Churches, neither have vicars, shall keep hospitality by their farmers or stewards, according as the Churches may bear, so that at the least-ways the extreme necessity of the poor parishioners be holpen and relieved, and such as passeth-by, preaching the words of God, may receive necessary bodily food, lest their Churches be forsaken of preachers through the violence of poverty : for the workman is worthy of his meat, neither any is bound to go a warfare at his own cost and charge.

CHAPTER IV.

In decimis et infra. Canon of John Stratford.

By approbation of this council we ordain *(statuimus)* that religious persons having ecclesiastical benefices within our province shall yearly distribute unto the poor parishioners of their benefices a certain quantity of alms, which shall be limited at the arbitrament of the ordinaries of the same places after the value of such benefices, whereunto they shall be compelled of their Bishops by pain of sequestration and subtraction of the fruits and profits of such benefices, until they obey competently in the premises.

TITULUS 5.

Of Prebends.

CHAPTER I.

Quia juxta sanctiones canonicas et infra.

Canon of Stephen.

We establish *(statuimus)* and, the holy council approving, we straitly inhibit, that henceforth no Church be committed unto many rulers, being all persons to be governed, but, whereas many persons be in one Church, we ordain that, as every one departeth, the portion of the deed shall increase and grow unto the living until the personages of that Church be come in to one only : neither many vicars hereafter shall be made in one Church, such Churches being excepted from this statute which have of old time been divided.

CHAPTER II.

Audistis et infra.   Canon of John Peccham.

According to the form of the general council we decree *(decernimus)* all benefices having care of souls, which they obtain in deed, that have not apostolic dispensation, for the plurality of such benefices, to be void by the law, through the receiving of that benefice which they last received. And albeit, he that so receiveth many benefices is deprived by the law from the last, after the rigour of the constitution of Lord Othobone, seeing that by the said constitution the institution is void by the law, we notwithstanding, intending to beware that we seem not to heap rigour upon rigour, and clearly perceiving and marking the mind and intent of the constitutions as well of the general council as of the Lord Othobone, whereof neither taketh away the benefices before obtained and also the last. But the general council taketh away only the forgotten and reserveth the last. And the constitution of Othobone decreeth the institution in the last to be void by the law, and yet taketh not away the forgotten by the law, wherefore we, as is said, mingling mercy with rigour, do permit, that he that hath forgotten, without the Pope's dispensation, many benefices with care of souls, shall be content with the last benefice so obtained according to the tenour of the general council, except perchance of raschenes[15] he strive to keep boldly the fore gotten also, in which case we judge him worthy neither of the first, neither of the last, no neither of any mean or other, but rather all to be void by the law, yea and all to be taken from him for ever, inasmuch as he keepeth them gotten in deed, but not gotten by the law, *et infra.* We also decree *(decernimus)* and for ever ordain that whosoever henceforth receive many benefices, all having care of souls, or otherwise incompatible without the Pope's dispensation, or get them by way of institution or commendam or custody, otherwise than the constitution of[a] Gregory made in the council of Lyons doth permit, the same in so doing to be deprived from all benefices that he hath so obtained, and moreover for so doing to be wrapped in the sentence of excommunication, from which he shall not obtain the gift of absolution, but only by us or our successors or by the apostolic see.

TITULUS 6.

Of institutions and commendams.

CHAPTER I.

Quia juxta et infra.   Canon of Stephen.

We ordain *(statuimus)* that no prelate, when he giveth Church or prebend, shall presume by any means to usurp

---

[a] De elec. nemo deinceps li. 6.

to himself the fruits of the said Church or prebend which
be not yet gathered, or shall dare extortly to take anything for the institution or putting in possession, or for
writing to be made thereof, or suffer his officials or Archdeacons anything so to take.

CHAPTER II.

Cum secundum Apostolum et infra.

Canon of Stephen.

If any be canonically presented unto a Church no man
speaking against it, we decree *(statuimus)* that the Bishop
shall in no means defer above two months to admit him
that is presented, so that he be able and meet: or also
whatsoever chanceth to be received of the same benefice
after the presentation, let it be restored unto him after he
is instituted as far forth as those fruits be come to the
Bishop's hands. The Archdeacon shall do likewise, if he
have been the cause, whereby he that was canonically
presented was not admitted within the said time, except
he propose to shew some reasonable cause before his
superior, when by him he shall be required for the same,
that is to say for what cause he did not admit him within
the time appointed by this Council.

CHAPTER III.

Ex solito cursu causarum et infra.

Constitution of John Peccham.

We ordain *(statuimus)* that every Bishop shall grant
and give unto the clerk whom he admitteth to a Church,
letters patent upon his admission, containing amongst
other things in what order he is, and by what title he is
admitted to such benefice.

CHAPTER IV.

Item quia Archidiaconi et infra.

Canon of John Stratford.

By approbation of this holy Council we ordain
(statuimus) that such as be bound, at the superior's

commandment, to induct them that be admitted to
ecclesiastical benefices, shall be contended for such their
inducting with moderate expenses, that is, if the Archdeacon induct, he shall be content with forty pence, if his
official, with two shillings a day for all his own expenses
and his waiters, putting him that shall be inducted nevertheless to his choice, whether he will provide for the
inductor and his servants in such quantity of money, or
else in other things necessary, if anything above this be
received of the inductors by occasion of the premises :
or else if they receive any more for the induction, or if it
happen them by any colour without cause reasonable to
defer their induction of the making of letters certificatory
or their deliverance to such as be inducted, we will them
that be culpable in this behalf to incur suspension from
office and Church entry in so doing, until all be restored
that is received contrary hereunto and full satisfaction be
made to him that is hurt through their fault in the
premises.

TITULUS 7.

Of the gift of Prebends.

Chapter I.

Ne lepra et infra.   Canon of Stephen.

We utterly think this an inconvenience, that, where one
is parson of a Church, there should anything in the same
Church be given unto another by his consent under the
name of a personage, except he that is parson already do
purely resign first the whole Church : we also ordain that
it shall not be lawful to any, whether he be patron, parson,
or vicar, to assign ought in the Church to any other under
the name of a benefice, as though it were lawful to keep
this with another benefice whereunto the care of souls is
annexed.

CHAPTER II.

A nostris majoribus et infra.   Canon of Boniface.

We ordain *(statuimus)* and make decree that the benefice of holy water shall be given to poor clerks. And for so much as we have heard that strife sometime hath risen betwixt the parsons and vicars of Churches and their parishioners upon the giving of such benefices (which strife as it is to us pleasant so ought we to cut away), we decree and ordain that the same parsons and vicars (to whom it more appertaineth to know which be apt and meet for such benefices) shall endeavour themselves to make such clerks in the said rooms as can and may conveniently serve and intend them in divine service after their minds, and will be obedient unto their commandments, from whom if the parishioners will frowardly withdraw the accustomed alms, let them diligently be monished to give them, yea, and if need be let them be straitly compelled by all manner ecclesiastical punishments.

CHAPTER III.

Esurientes avarifiae et infra.   Canon of John Stratford.

By foresight of this present Council we statute *(statuimus)* that whatsoever clerks hereafter do procure themselves to be presented unto dignity, parsonage, office, or prebend, or to any other ecclesiastical benefice, being yet full and possessed in deed by other, or cause any such to be given unto them by any manner person, and afterwards directly or indirectly by virtue of brief, *quare non admisit,* or *quare impedit,* or any other like, do sue against the Bishops or other in secular Court making no mention in the said briefs of the unlawful possessioners of such benefices, and that they have been lawfully called before their ordination and yet not removed, shall incur in the deed doing the sentence of the great excommunication, and so being excommunicated in no means shall be admitted to such benefices, but shall be counted unable for ever unto them, except they first cause inquisitions to be made at the ordinaries' commandments upon the causes of the pretended vacations, and also cause the possessioners *canonically*[a] to be amoved by the ecclesiastical judges competent in that behalf : but if any contrary to this be instituted or admitted in fact to a benefice possessed by another, such institution or admission shall lack effect in the law. And whosoever doth so institute or admit either by his own right, either by right committed unto him any so presented, the possessioner of that benefice (by sufficient authority and sententially in ecclesiastical court first not removed) know he himself so long to be suspended from office and benefice, until the benefice with all damages and losses be restored unto the possessioner as congruity requireth. And he that so is instituted or admitted, if he suffer himself to be inducted, contrary to this statute, in a benefice obtained by another, shall be taken as intruded and shall incur in the deed doing the penalties of intrusion which be contained in the Constitution of Othobone, whose beginning is *amoris proprii,* and all other penalties decreed by the canons and holy Fathers : notwithstanding we intend not through the premises to derogate the power of ordinaries, but that they may give the benefices appertaining to their collation, whosoever be possessed in fact and not by the law, neither by this constitution will we bind them that admit the collation of their benefices.

TITULUS 8.

Of Church goods not to be alienated.

CHAPTER I.

Ecclesiarum indemnitatibus.   Canon of Stephen.

That the Churches indemnities may be provided for by authority of this present Council we ordain *(duximus statuendum)* that no Abbot or Prior, no Archdeacon or Dean, or other having parsonage or dignity, neither any

[a] i.e., not by violence, but by process to show, etc.

inferior clerk presume to sell pledge or mortgage or to give in fee of new, or any other wise to alienate to his kin or friends, or to any other, the possessions or profits of dignity or Church that is committed to them, the form and manner of the canons therein not observed. And if any dare do contrary to this, both the thing that is done shall be of no value. And also he that doth it shall be deprived by his superior from dignity or parsonage or Church which he hath so hurt, except he will at his own cost, without the Church damages, call back again that he hath alienated within certain time prefixed by his superior. And he also, that hereafter receiveth the Church goods or, after he is warned, presumeth to withhold them, shall be stricken with the sword of excommunication, and in no wise shall be healed of that wound until he hath made restitution, the same thing also shall the greater prelates observe and keep.

Chapter II.

Ut secundum canonicas sanctiones. Canon of Stephen.

We will *(volumus)* that the prelates of religious houses, neither sell, neither freely give, to clerks or lay, corrodies[16] or stipends for ever or for a time, except urgent necessity require it, and the diocesan thereunto consent.

TITULUS 9.

Of letting out and hiring.

Chapter I.

Ut vere videamur et infra.　　　Canon of Stephen.

We ordain *(statuimus)* that such Churches as be deputed to certain persons be let to farm to none without a just cause approved by the Bishop, and then by his consent to be let to some persons within orders, which may be thought to bestow the Church's fruits in good uses.

Chapter II.

Vendentes et infra.   Canon of John Peccham.

Churches may not be let to farm but to men of the Church of pure life and honesty, which the Bishops of that part may freely correct and order, and in such letting it must be provided that a good portion agreeable to the law, which is the fourth part, be assigned by the Bishop's arbitrament out of such farms to be faithfully distributed to the poor parishioners, so that four credible persons of the same parish may witness it truly to be done. And that all feigned and coloured bargains may be excluded from such outlettings and farms by which the Churches be granted, and the farms letten to the lay in the persons of clerks falsely surmised, or under the name of the holy water clerk, we ordain, the holy Council approving the same, that, if any clerk be found in such craft, he shall be punished according to the statute of Lord Othobone, yea and more grievously if the prelates think it expedient.

Chapter III.

Licet bonae memoriae et infra.

Canon of John Stratford.

By approbation of this provincial Council, we add *(adjicienda statuimus)* unto the constitutions that be made before, ordaining that as oft as any ecclesiastical benefices of our province from this time forward is let to farm to a clerk and a lay, or the name of a lay is put with the name of a clerk in the instruments made upon such lease, or a clerk is feigned to be the farmer when in deed he is not, or else if any lay gather in their own name the fruits, rents and provents of benefices let to farm, and convert them directly into their own uses, such contracts shall not hold, nor either party shall be bound to other, but, as well the letters as the receivers of benefices, henceforth after that manner we will to be punished (the addition of the clerk's name notwithstanding) by losing the third part of the provents of the benefice to let, or the

H

value thereof to be paid to both (if both be able) or else
of the letter (if the receiver be not able) unto the Cathedral Church of that place. And because religious persons
and others which have ecclesiastical benefices of our
Province unto their own proper uses, affirm themselves
not to be bound by the said constitutions, by consent of
this present council we ordain that if they let to farm such
benefices, or their portion of tithes and provents which
they receive in them by virtue of appropriation, to clerks,
the diocesan's licence not obtained, or by any means to
lay people, or howsoever contrary to the tenour of this
present constitution or other, they shall henceforth suffer
the same penalty.

TITULUS 10.

Of Gages.

Inhibemus, ne pignus.   Canon of Edmund.

We forbid any man to strive or contend to keep the
gage,[17] after he have received the principal debt of the
fruits of the said gage, above all expenses for its usury.

TITULUS 11.

Of Donations.

Cordis dolore concutimur et infra.
                                Canon of John Stratford.

By deliberation of this present Council we will that all
and singular in our Province, which, having any likely
conjecture of death to draw nigh, do presume to give all
their goods or any notable quantity of them amongst the
living, or make any other alienation of evil purpose or
fraud, so that the Church, the King or other creditors
unto whom the said givers or alienators were effectually
bound should be defrauded of their rights, or their wives
or children should be defrauded without recovery of their
portions due unto them either by law or custom.

Secondarily, all such as attend the sick at their last end and all other times, if they counsel or temourously procure such donations or alienations to be made, and all such as withdraw the sick or other by counsel or evil suasions by the mind of testament making, by means whereof certain it is that the free testament making is let and the Church and other above named be maliciously stopped from their right.

Thirdly, all such as be of knowledge and consent of the said fraud or malice, and all that receive the things so given or alienated, or give counsel or favour thereunto shall incur in the deed doing the sentence of the great excommunication. And not only that, but also they that so give or alien such their goods within our province for their great and weighty offence shall lack ecclesiastical sepulture, any manner absolution given from the said sentence notwithstanding. And lest the difficulty of proving the said fraud or malicious purpose should make our provision without profit or effect, we statute *(statuimus)* and ordain that as often as any of the said Province shall either give goods as aforesaid, or otherwise by any title alienate them whole, or in so notable quantity that it may appear that of the residue the Church and other creditors cannot be satisfied of their duties, and their wives and children of their said portions as it is becoming, so often the said donation or alienation shall be judged in that deed to be made by fraud or some malicious intent, no further proof thereof required.

TITULUS 12.

Of the peculiar or proper of Clerks.

Quia plerique et infra.   Canon of Stephen.

By expedient foresight we decree *(decernimus)* that clerks beneficed may not bestow the Churches fruits in lay fee or presume to buy houses or lay possessions or build houses in lay fee for their concubines or children, or minister money to buy such with for their need, that by

this means occasion of evil doing may be taken away :
and if any be suspected upon just causes herein, except he
purge himself at the superior's judgment, he shall be
punished at the superior's discretion.

TITULUS 13.

Of Testaments.

CHAPTER I.

Ut clericalis et infra.   Canon of Stephen.

Although we would that the lawful testaments of
beneficed clerks which depart should be kept, yet will we
not that ought should be left by testament to their concubines, but if there be, the whole to be converted at the
Bishop's discretion unto the use of that Church which the
dead ruled.

CHAPTER II.

Cum viris religiosis.   Canon of Stephen.

Forasmuch as religious persons may not by the law
possess anything proper which, at their entry into religion,
gave both themself and also all that they had at once
unto God, we presently define *(definimus)* that no person,
being in regular order, may presume to make testament
saying he hath no temporal thing of his own, whereof he
may make another the owner.

CHAPTER III.

Religiosa sinceritas et infra.   Canon of John Peccham.

Where it is well provided by certain statute made at
Lambeth that no religious persons, of whatsoever profession they be, may be the executors of testaments but by
the will and licence of the ordinaries, we adding more
thereunto do ordain that no religious shall be suffered to
be the executors of any testament, except his superiors
will pledge or be bound for him that he shall sufficiently
execute, giving a full and faithful reckoning of the

residue if any be, and also, without any sticking, shall make answer to the ordinary of that place for losses and damages if any through him shall arise. And because that certain which bear the habit of religion, although they be not made executors, be made nevertheless, sometime of their own head, and sometime by the foolishness of other, the distributors of the dead's goods, whereof we see great hurt and losses to come unto such goods, therefore we command the same thing to be observed about such distribution as is before provided for the execution, forbidding them under the pain of anathema, that is eternal damnation, otherwise to meddle with such execution or distribution : wherefore such as cannot give sufficient caution know they that by determination of this present Council themselves to be excluded as well from execution as distribution of such goods for ever.

CHAPTER IV.

Item quia locorum.　　　Canon of Simon Mepham.

Also because the ordinaries of places, hath been hitherto (as it is reported) very heavy and costly *unto the executors of testaments,* by seeking out delays, crafts and cautels, about the insinuation[18] of testaments, and committing of the administration, to the intent they might the rather milk them of their money, we ordain that for the insinuation of a poor man's testament whose inventory passeth not a £5 sterling, nothing in the world shall be required.

CHAPTER V.

Statutum bonae memoriae.　　Canon of John Stratford.

Calling to mind the statute made by Boniface of good memory, once Archbishop of Canterbury, our predecessor, concerning the goods of them that die intestate and the last wills of ascripts and of other men of servile condition whose beginning is *Ceterum contingit interdum etc.,* which statute of late is called into doubt by many men, we therefore (some things added unto the same and some things taken away as it appeareth by the words ensuing) do ordain the same firmly hereafter to be observed and kept, but it happeneth sometimes that when lay people and clerks, by the hand and judgment of God, depart intestate, the lords of the feods will not suffer the debts of the dead to be paid of their movable goods, neither will suffer the said goods to be distributed in the uses of their wives their children or parents, or that portion which after the custom of the country appertaineth to the dead, otherwise to be bestowed for them at the disposition of the ordinaries. Other there be that letteth, or causeth to be let, the free making of testaments and their executions, and the last wills of ascripts and of other persons of servile condition, of women also both married and unmarried and of their own wives and of other men's wives, which things they do as well against the laws as against the customs of the Church hitherto approved, unto the displeasure of the divine majesty and evident hurt and injury of the Church's rights, therefore by authority of this present Council we decree *(decernimus)* all and singular, that hereafter offend in these things or any of them, to be wrapped in the sentence of the great excommunication : moreover, when testaments be approved and allowed before the ordinaries of the places (to whom it appertaineth), the proving or allowing of such testaments shall in no wise be required or called again of the lay judges, except it be by reason of lay fee, if any happen to be bequeathed in a testament : neither clerks nor lay of whatsoever condition they be shall hinder or let, but that the testaments and last wills of the dead may go forward and take effect in such things as may be bequeathed by custom or law. And if there be any that dare do hereafter contrary to these things know they themselves to fall into the sentence of the great court by authority of this present Council. And against them and other which work wickedly in the premises we decree the spiritual sword to be exercised as against violators and disturbers of the Church's liberties. We forbid also any executor of testaments to be suffered to minister the goods of any testator, except a true inventory be first made of the said goods, the funeral expenses and such as shall be spent about the making of such inventory only excepted. And we will this inventory to be delivered to the ordinaries of the places within the time appointed by their discretions, and, after that the testament be proved before the ordinaries according to the manner, the execution, or administration of such goods shall not be committed unto any but such as can and (if need require) do give sufficient caution and faithful promise to make a due reckoning of their administration, when they shall be conveniently required thereunto by the ordinaries of the places. Also we ordain by authority of this present Council that no religious persons of whatsoever profession they be, may be executors of testaments, except it be granted by the will and licence of their ordinaries and the parish Church receive his accustomed duty of the portion that appertaineth to the dead, we ordain moreover that no executor may take or appropriate unto himself anything of the dead's goods whose testament he executeth either by title of buying, or any other title but that is given unto him of the testator being alive, or is left in his testament or last will, or is approved at the ordinaries' discretion for the labour of the executor, or was owed unto him by the dead, or is due for moderate expenses of his administration, under pain of suspension from Church entry, into which we will them that do the contrary to incur in so doing, whereof they shall not obtain absolution until they have restored the things so taken or unjustly appropriated, and have paid of their own goods unto the fabric of the Cathedral Church, whereof the dead was subject double the things which they so take or appropriate. All and singular the above written we command solemnly to be published twice every year in every Church throughout our province of Canterbury.

CHAPTER VI.

Ita quorundam et infra.   Canon of John Stratford.

We ordain *(statuimus)* that Bishops and other inferior ecclesiastical judges of our province of Canterbury shall in no wise by any craft or colour meddle with the goods of clerks beneficed, which may by the custom of England make their testament, or with the goods of any other testator except it be in cases expressly permitted, but he shall suffer the executors of their testaments freely to dispose and order the same. And the goods of them that die intestate such as remain after the debts paid they shall dispose and distribute in charitable deeds for the soul's health of the dead, and unto such persons as were kin, servants, or neighbours of the dead, or such other, retaining nothing thereof to themselves (except it seem reasonable something to be retained for the ordinaries' labour) under pain of suspension from Church entry wherein we will ecclesiastical judges doing the contrary to incur in so doing until they have made competent satisfaction in the premises.

CHAPTER VII.

Adeo quorundam et infra.   Canon of John Stratford.

We ordain *(statuimus)* that, for the proving or allowing or insinuation of any manner of testaments, there shall nothing in the world be received by the Bishops or other ordinaries: notwithstanding we grant the clerks that write such insinuations to receive for their labour only sixpence, but if the inventory of any dead's goods be found to pass the sum of thirty shillings, and yet cometh not to £5, the Bishops or ordinaries or their deputies and the auditors of accounts or other ministers intending such accounts may not presume to take above 12d. for the account, hearing and all things to be done about the same, or for letters of acquaintance or any other, but if the said inventories contain the sum of £5

or more and yet under £20, they that intend the counts
and other ministers aforesaid shall be contented with
three shillings for their labour for the letters of acquaintance and for other things above rehearsed. And if they
contain £20 or more and yet less than £60, they shall not
take above five shillings for their labours, letters and
other writings : but if such inventories come to the sum
of £40 or more and yet not to a £100 they may receive
ten shillings for the premises and not above. And if the
said inventories contain the sum of £100 or more and
yet not £150 they shall not presume to take for the
premises above twenty shillings and so ascending or proceeding farther for every fifty rising they may receive
ten shillings over and beside the said twenty shillings and
not above : notwithstanding we permit to the clerks to
take for every letter of acquaintance that they write
above the letters beforesaid sixpence for their labour.
And if it chance that any of them do take in any case
aforewritten by any manner or cautel, couen or craft,
above the sum taxed, whether it be ready money or other
things, he shall be bound to give within a month towards
the works of the Cathedral Church of that place double
that which is received above duty, or else if they be
Bishops that differ above the said time to restore the said
double, know they that Church entry is forbidden them.
And if they be inferior ordinaries, they shall be suspended
from office and benefice until they make full payment of
such double to the said Cathedral Churches. And in no
wise letters of acquaintance shall be granted or given to
the executors of testaments in the time of their probation,
allowing, or insinuation, or afterwards, before the
executors have made a faithful account of their administration, under pain of suspension from Church entry by
the space of six months, into which we will them that do
the contrary to incur in so doing.

TITULUS 14.

Of Sepultures.

CHAPTER I.

Quia saepe et infra.   Canon of John Stratford.

We enact and ordain *(statuimus)* through our Province that hereafter, when men of the Church have done Diriges and other service for the dead, none shall be received into the private houses (where the bodies oftentimes do rest until burying time) to keep night watches as they use, the friends and kinfolk of the dead only excepted, and such as perchance will say psalms for the dead, under pain of the great excommunication, which sentence both they that keep watches contrary to the premises and they also that receive them have a good cause to fear.

CHAPTER II.

Quia inter Rectores.   Canon of Robert Winchelsea.

Because we much desire to quench the strifes which often rise betwixt the parsons of Churches and their parishens, we make and ordain *(statuimus)* that, if he that departeth have in goods three beasts at the least or more of whatsoever kind they be (the best reserved for him that ought to have it) the next best shall be that Church's where he received the sacraments while he lived.

TITULUS 15.

Of Parishes and strange Parishens.

CHAPTER I.

Adinstar Patrisfamilias.

According to the example of the goodman of the house, spoken of in the gospel which sent forth many workmen into his vineyard, to the intent that the diligent labour of many might bring to pass that one could not do, we sententially define *(definimus)* that in every parish

Church where the parish is large and wide, there be two or three priests according to the greatness of the parish and the power or value of the Church, lest peradventure, while one priest is sick or weak (which thing God forbid), divine service be taken from them that would gladly hear it or the sacraments of the Church be denied them that be sick.

CHAPTER II.

Altissimus de terra et infra.   Canon of John Peccham.

None may give Church rights unto another priest's diocesan without his manifest licence, which ordinance we intend not to stretch unto pilgrims and palmers *(peregrinantes)* or to derogate the case of necessity thereby.

TITULUS 16.
Of Tithes and Oblations.

CHAPTER I.

Quia quidam maledictionis. Canon of Simon Mepham.

Forasmuch as there be certain cursed children, whereof one sort have gone about to diminish the devotion of the people, and to refrain them to the offering of one penny or some other small quantity at the solemnities of marriage, of women's purifications, of minds for the dead, and such other, in which solemnities the Lord Himself (in the persons of his ministers) was wont to be honoured of his people through the receiving of their oblations : and the residue which the faithful were wont to offer they have often times applied to their own uses or others at their pleasure : and another sort, not regarding how the Lord omnipotent (whose the earth is and the fullness thereof and all that dwell therein) hath commandeth the tenth to be given to Him in sign and token of His universal dominion and lordship, and hath appointeth the same to His clerks for serving Him : doth sometimes maliciously stop and let the men of the Church

unto whom the receiving of tithes doth appertain, or their
servants, or at the least do cause or procure them to be
letted, so that they cannot freely go and come in to the
grounds where the tithes grow, to gather them together,
to keep them, or to carry them whither they would.
Another sort also carry away such tithes and consume
them or else cause them to be carried and consumed, or
do some manner of hurt in them, or causeth it to be done,
except there be gloves, hose or such other gifts given or
promised unto them, we therefore minding to set up a
good remedy against the damnable sorts of such
mischievous people, will make no new statute in this
behalf, but will set forth statutes of the old canons
against all and every such instigator's letters, withstanders
and other beforesaid, through whose wicked crafts any
hurt is done to the Churches or their parsons, vicars or
ministers, or any honour or profit accustomed is
diminished. And by the authority of this present Council,
we declare and pronounce all and singular that hereafter
offend in the premises, or in any point of them, to be
wrapped in the bonds of the great excommunication, from
the which they shall not be loosed (except in the point of
death) but by their diocesan, and that when, through their
labour, the people's devotion is effectually restored again
to the Churches and full satisfaction made to the
ministers of the Church for all hurts and trespacese
(*excessibus*).

CHAPTER II.

Erroris damnabilis.   Canon of John Stratford.

Men are so blinded in the way of damnable error that
they eschew not the destruction of their own souls, while
they give to them that cut down their corn the tenth garbe
for their labour, and then accounting not the same but
under this error of reckoning and casting, do pay to the
Church the eleventh garbe for the tenth affirming that
they may pay of the corn not tenthed the wages of their
hired servants for their harvest labour specially before

the time of tithing come. And by this means do despise the commandments of the old and new Testaments. The superstitious malice also of some lay persons hath newly invented that, when they have left in their grounds certain tithable garbes and yet not marked for the tenth and the spiritualty, men's servants do take and carry away in the name of tithing the said garbes or other things of the tenth part so left, they straight cry out and call them thieves, and cause them to be arrested or attacked as thieves, and do hurt and divers ways trouble both the said servants and their masters for the carrying and taking away such tithes. And also certain of the said lay people, because the same tithes of garbe and hay or other things be carried over and upon their grounds, sue the spiritual men and their ministers in the secular court and weary them with great labours and expenses. Moreover there be that set and appoint the wages and carriages into the fields and from the fields in places of evil and cumbrous carriage and by long circuits, and will suffer them to carry the tithes and bring their carriage only by these ways with great difficulty, contrary to the Church's liberty. And some when they have cast out the garbes and marked them for the tenth, yet they will not suffer them to be carried from their ground as long as any of the blade remaineth in them, but wittingly do suffer their own and others beasts to break and consume them, and do make divers stops, lets and impediments, and also cause and procure many stops to be made, about the paying, gathering and away carrying of the same tithes, unto the great hurt and manifest prejudice of the liberties and rights of the Church and the jeopardy of their souls. Therefore we being desirous to provide a good remedy against the labour and damnable boldness of such wicked persons, by deliberation of this present Council we pronounce all and every that hereafter offend in the premises or any thereof, within our Province, or command the unlawful foresaid things or any part of them to be done, or in anywise procure them, or ratify them when they be done in their name, furthermore all and singular such as work wicked inventions and deceits by the which the rights, or approbated customs, or the liberties of the Church be in any thing diminished or suffer any injury, damage or griefs contrary to the Church's liberty, to be wrapped in the bonds of the great excommunication, their absolution reserved specially to their diocesan, the point of death only excepted.

CHAPTER III.

Quanquam exsolventibus.   Canon of John Stratford.

Albeit God hath promised abundance of all fruit and fatness of possessions unto all that pay their tithes well and truly yet (with grievous heart we speak it) there be of our Province, which contrary to the doctrine of the old and new Testaments doth refuse and deny to pay tithes to God and the Church unto which they be notably due, of their coppices and lopped woods and trees, in which there is less cost bestowed them in the fruits of the field, thinking that they may now lawfully deny to pay them, seeing they have not beforetime been paid, and so do take it for a law which hath grown up by long custom, calling into doubt moreover what ought to be judged coppice wood : wherefore we perceiving that, though the Church hath been long defrauded of her portion, yet the fault is not thereby diminished but rather augmented, and that hunger, penury and neediness of all things doth oppress them that pay not well and truly their tithes, by provision of this Council we declare *(declaramus)* and will that to be taken for coppice wood, which is kept and nourished to be cut, of whatsoever kind of trees it be and, after it is cut, doth grow again from the stocks and roots. And that tithe real and predial[19] ought to be paid of the same unto the parish and mother Churches.   And also that all possessions of such woods shall be compelled by all punishment of the Church to pay tithes of all wood cut in them likewise as they do of hay and blade.

Chapter IV.

Immoderatae temeritatis et infra.

Canon of John Stratford.

We do decree *(decernimus)* with full declaration of this present Council that all manner lay men which under pretext of any manner deed custom or any manner colour do occupy, take, or any wise dispose the oblations made or hereafter to be made in the honour of God in Churches, chapels, or their porches or lettens, or in any other place within our Province, to stand in so doing under sentence of the great curse, except it be done with the consent of the spiritual persons to whom the receipt of such oblations doth appertain, and for a sufficient and lawful cause approved first by the Bishop of that place.

Chapter V.

Quoniam propter diversas.

Canon of Robert Winchelsea.

Forasmuch as through diverse customs in asking tithes, debates and strifes, occasions of evil and great hatreds oftentimes doth rise in divers Churches betwixt the parsons and their parishens, therefore we will and ordain *(volumus et statuimus)* that, in all Churches throughout the Province of Canterbury, there be one fashion and form of tithes and other spiritual profits. First, we will that the tenth of fruits be paid wholly, without diminution or deduction of expenses, as well of the fruits of trees as of all manner seeds and herbs of gardens, except the parishens sufficiently redeem such tithes : also we will and ordain that tithe of hay be required wheresoever it grow, whether it be in great or in small meadows, or in chimynes[a] and that they be paid as the profit of the Church shall require. And as touching the bringing up of cattle as of lambs, we ordain that for six lambs and under, six halfpence be given for tithe, if there be seven lambs in number the seventh shall be the parsons for his

[a] i.e., roadside grass.

tithe, so that the parson which hath received the seventh
lamb pay three pence in recompense unto the parishen
of whom he hath received the lamb, and he that receiveth
the eighth shall give one penny and the ninth a halfpenny
to his parishen, or if the parson will rather, let him tarry
to another year, till he may receive the tenth lamb in full
number. And he that so doth tarry, shall require the
second best lamb, or at the least the third best of the
second year, and that for the forbearing of the first year.
And so is it to be understood of the tenth of wool, but if
the sheep be nourished in one place in the winter, and
another place in the summer, the tenth must be divided,
likewise if any man buy or sell sheep in the mid-time,
being certain from what parish the sheep came, the tenth
must be divided as it is in that thing that followeth two
dwelling places, but, if it be uncertain from what parish
they come, let that Church have the whole tenth within
whose bounds they be at shear time : as concerning milk
we will the tithe to be paid of the cheese in his time and
of the milk in autumn and winter, except the parishens
will make a competent redemption for such and that
according to the value of the tenth, and for the Church's
profit : of the provents of mills we will the tenth to be
paid fully and faithfully : of pastures and closes as well
common as not common, we ordain that tithe be faithfully paid, and that after the number of the cattle and
days, as it is profitable to the Church, we statute and
ordain that tithe be required and paid in due manner of
all manner fishing and bees, as it is of other goods justly
gotten which renew every year : we also decree personal
tithes to be paid of artificers and merchants of their
getting in their business, likewise of carpenters, smiths,
masons, weavers, innkeepers and of all other workmen
and labourers and such as serve for wages : we will that
they give the tenth of their wages, unless the same will
give a certain towards the works or lights of the Church
if it shall so please the parson.

In requiring the principal legacy that is a mortuary we
will the custom of that parish or diocese which the

Church is possessed of to be observed and kept, so that whether he be parson or vicar or yearly chaplain, he have God before his eyes in the asking and requiring thereof, but inasmuch as there be many that will not willingly pay tithes, we statute that the parochians be monished once, twice and thrice to pay to God and the Church. And so at length let them be driven thereunto by ecclesiastical censures if need require. And if they desire to be released or absolved from the said suspension, first let them send to the ordinary of that place to be absolved and in due manner to be punished. And the parsons or vicars or yearly chaplains named parish priests, which either by fear or favour of man without regard of the fear of God, do not ask and require with effect the tithes in manner aforesaid, shall stand suspended until such season, until they have paid half a mark of silver unto the Archdeacon of that place for their inobedience.

CHAPTER VI.

Quoniam ut audivimus.   Canon of Robert Winchelsea.

Inasmuch as many and diverse contentions doth rise (as we here), upon the tithes and raising up of cattle, betwixt the parsons of Churches, through the removing of cattle in divers parishes at divers seasons of the year, we willing to prepare the way of peace do define and ordain, that in whatsoever parish the sheep do continually lie and feed from shear time, unto the feast of S. Martin in winter, the tithe of wool, milk and cheese of that time shall be paid whole to the same parish, although they be removed from thence and be shorn in another. And lest craft should be wrought in the said case, we command that before the sheep be removed from their pasture or otherwise taken away, the parsons of the Churches be assured for the payment of the tithe, but, if they be removed to divers parishers within the said time, every Church shall receive the tenth according to the rate of the time, so that less space than thirty days be not accounted, but if they lie in one parish and feed continually in another

I

throughout the said time, let the tenth be divided betwixt them. And if they be brought after the feast of S. Martin to strange feeding and until shear time be fed in one, or else divers parishes, whether it be in the owner's pasture, or else in any others, a regard taken after the number of the sheep, let that feeding be estimed and after the estimation of their feeding let tithes be required of their owner. As for the tenth of milk and cheese coming of kine and goats, it must be paid where they lie and feed, or else if they lie in one parish and feed in another the tithe shall be divided betwixt the parsons. And lambs, calves, colts and other like increase titheable, shall be tithed after consideration of the time as they tarried in divers places where they ingendered, and where they fell, and where they were nourished, but what shall be paid for the tithe where the milk through the fewness of kine or sheep is not sufficient to make cheese, and what for lambs, calves, goats, flyses of wool, gese, or such other, of the which the tenth cannot certainly be assigned for their fewness, we judge it to be left to the custom of the place. Also we command that in case any man kill sheep after S. Martin's Day, or by any day chance the sheep die, he omit not to pay to the Parish Church the due tithe. And if any strange sheep be shorn in another parish the tithe shall be paid to the parson there, except it can be sufficiently shewed that such satisfaction is made for the tithe in another place, that it may lawfully stop the payment to be made there.

CHAPTER VII.

Sancta ecclesia et infra.   Canon of Robert Winchelsea.

Whereas by the commandment of scripture tithes ought to be paid fully and without diminution of all things that spring of new through the year no time excused. And is also lawful to every parish priest, parson, or vicar to compel their parishens by censures of the Church to pay their tithes, we command *(mandamus)*, enjoining under virtue of obedience all and singular parsons, vicars, and

parish priests, with all curates of Parish Churches
throughout our diocese, that they diligently monish and
with effect cause, and every one in his parish monish and
cause, that all and singular the said parishens pay fully
and without diminution unto their Churches the tithes
under specified, that is to say the tithe of milk from the
first time of renewing as well in the month of August as
other months. Also of the profits that riseth of woods
and trees, as by fatting of swine if it be sold, of fish
stewes or ponds, or other fishing in running or standing
waters, of trees, of beasts, of doves, of seeds, of fruit,
and all manner warm beasts of fowling, of gardens, of
curtilages, of wool, of linen, of wine, and grain, of turfs,
in those places wherein they be made and digged, of
swans, of capons of gese and of ducks, of eggs, of hedge-
rows, of bees, of honey and wax, of mills, of huntings, of
all crafts and merchandise, also of lambs, of calves, of
colts after their value, and of all provents of other things,
from henceforth that they make competent satisfaction
unto the Churches to the which they be bound without
deduction of expenses except in crafts and merchandise.
And if they refuse to obey their monitions, let them
compel them to pay the said tithes by sentence of suspension excommunication and interdiction.

TITULUS 17.
Of Regulars and such as enter Religion.
CHAPTER I.
Quia vero nonnunquam et infra.   Canon of Stephen.

None shall be admitted monks before the age of
eighteen years, except an urgent or evident necessity or
profit cause otherwise.

CHAPTER II.
Sancti-moniales plurimae et infra.
Canon of John Peccham.

Some nuns be so far deceived that, when they be of
lawful age and discretion, after they have lived like nuns

above an year amongst nuns, they think that they be not professed, and that they may lawfully return to the world, only because they have not received the Bishop's blessings with solemnity of their vow promised : we putting away such error, by authority of this present council do declare them to be accounted professed indeed after they have willingly led a regular life about a year in the company of regulars, so much that they may not be suffered to return to the world, but yet they shall be consecrated or covered by the Bishops with due solemnity in their time. The same we judge of monks and all other religious, as much as appertaineth to the bond of profession, which have no canonical impediment, and have had upon them above a year willingly the habit of religion in any monastery; and that habit cast off be gone again to the world, like apostates to be repelled from all manner ecclesiastical benefices, and shall be compelled by the order of the law to go again to their monasteries, for which sort we will diligent inquisition, and search to be made by the Archdeacons, for we know that many such do cloke wolfs' minds under a lamb's skin.

TITULUS 18.

Of Vows and redeeming of Vows.

CHAPTER I.

Quia juxta scripturae.   Canon of Stephen.

Because, according to the witness of scripture, we be bound to pay to God such vows as we healthfully make, we declare *(decernimus)* this to be added that Bishops cause twice in an year the form of profession made in their consecration diligently to be read before them, that they may the better remember their promise the oftener that it soundeth in their ears.

CHAPTER II.

Praecipimus ut sacerdotes.   Canon of Edmund.

We command *(praecipimus)* that priests oft monish the people, and specially the women, that they make not their vows but with deliberation, and with the consent of their husbands and the counsel of priests.

TITULUS 19.

Of the state of Regulars.

CHAPTER I.

Ut rectius gerantur.   Canon of Stephen.

That all things may the better be ordered, which no doubt shall be if the administration of exterior and outward things be done accordingly for the quietness of the cloisterers, we decree *(statuimus)* and ordain that as well the under ministers of things of the monastery as the chiefs heads four times, or at the least twice, in the year shall give account of all receipts and expenses before certain of their brethren deputed by the convent to the same purpose, or else before their superiors according to the custom of the monastery hereunto : we will not such prelates to be bound as have their possessions separate from their monks or canons.

CHAPTER II.

Quia nonnunquam serpens antiquus.
                                    Canon of Stephen.

Forasmuch as the old serpent which continually lieth in waiting against holy men often seasons the more solitary, and, without comforting the one the other, he findeth them the sooner, he overcasteth and confounded them by his assaults, by circumspect deliberation we ordain *(statuimus)* that as well monks as canons regular and nuns shall sleep and rest together in one dorter every one having his bed assigned to himself only. They shall also eat together in one refectory, and shall not have their meat prepared every one by himself, but jointly and in common for all : neither money shall be given to every one for his raiment, but all such things shall be diligently ordered by certain persons deputed for the same to minister clothing as the goods and faculties of the house may bear. And when they deliver new raiment let them receive the old and turn them in to the use of poor men or other necessities, and that by the counsel of the Abbot or Abbess, for it shall not be lawful to the said deputy, to deliver any monk, or canon, or nun money or other thing for his raiment, neither shall it be lawful to monk, canon, or nun to receive any such, and, if they do, the said officer shall be deposed, and the monk or canon or nun shall lack their new garments that year.

CHAPTER III.

Ad haec quoniam sexum muliebrem.

Canon of Stephen.

Moreover inasmuch as it is necessary effectually to strength with many remedies the nature and kind of women which otherwise is very weak against the craftiness of the old enemy, we decree and ordain *(decernimus)* that nuns and other women dedicated to the service of God shall not have veils or wimples of silk, neither shall dare to bear in their veils needles of silver or gold, neither they nor monks or canons regular shall have silken girdles garnished with gold or silver, neither shall they wear from henceforth burnet cloth or any other irregular colour, they shall also measure their garments after their bodies so that their garments exceed not the length of their bodies, but let them be content to wear a garment, as Joseph did, that commonly covereth their feet. And only a nun professed may wear a ring, and let her be content with one : if any dare do contrary to this prohibition, and they warned do not amend, he or she shall be corrected according to the discipline of their rules.

Chapter IV.

Ut Secundum Canonicas.   Canon of Stephen.

To the intent that the multitude of witnesses may be a record unto Abbots of their honest conversation, which according to the canons ought to be a rule of living unto the younger, we therefore decree that they change their chaplains, or at the least one of them, every year, and he that hath but one shall change the same, except there be a necessary cause to the contrary, so that if any slander of their life (which God forbid) happen to rise, to the more their life is known, the more witnesses there may be of their innocence.

Chapter V.

Inhibemus ne moniales.   Canon of Stephen.

We forbid nuns to receive secular women, but only necessary servants to inhabit within the compass of their houses except their diocesan thereunto assent. Also we command silence to be kept, in place and time appointed, as well of monks as of canons and nuns, neither shall it be lawful for men or women to go forth of the compass of their house without licence of their superior, which shall not be granted without a certain cause and honest, so that no cloisterer shall go forth for cause of recreation or to visit his parents, except he be such as no evil can or may be suspected, who shall also always have with him a fellow. And as often as licence is granted to any to go forth, a certain day shall be appointed of his homecoming. This we will also to be observed that if the Bishop, or Abbot, or the conventual Prior having no Abbot, shall think it expedient that any offender tarry for a time in another place, that he be sent to another house of the same religion within the same Bishopric, or if it be necessary within another Bishopric. And the Diocesan shall compel him to be admitted, who shall be in all things there subjected to regular discipline, so that if, through his abode, the place where he tarrieth be much charged, another of that house shall be sent to tarry in the monastery of the transgressor, which shall not be received into his own house again, before he have full repented his fault, and then let him be called home by his superior : but if the monastery where the offender tarrieth send none in his stead unto his monastery, the offender shall have his clothing from his own place.

CHAPTER VI.

Omnen autem singularitatem.   Canon of Stephen.

We forbid all singularity in their refectory, that is to say that meat be not prepared otherwise for one than for another, but he that is chief shall provide sometimes such things to be ordained for himself wherewith he may succour and help the weakness and sickness of others, as it shall seem expedient. We will also all manner of victual for religious persons to be set before them without any subtraction, as well in their convent as elsewhere they be refreshed : and that that is left (of the whole set before them) to go to the almose without diminution to be given to the poor by the amner, so that neither the Abbot, neither the Prior nor Amner may otherwise order it. And whosoever will not admit or keep this statute or that statute concerning raiment let him be suspended, if he be a priest, from celebrating divine service : if he be of inferior orders or a nun from the receiving of Christ's Body until full satisfaction be made. Also we forbid all nuns to eat flesh by themselves in such refectories where they were not wont to eat flesh. Moreover we will no monks to be admitted into another's monastery for fellowship or other consideration without the letters of his Bishop or Abbot, or Prior conventual having none Abbot, which thing we will to be observed amongst canons regular and nuns. Let the Bishops also provide that nuns may be sustained in all things necessary with the goods of their monastery and suffer none to be admitted above their number, or any to be received after they be once brought to their number. And this we firmly decree by the

authority of this present Council.   And, if it happen hereafter any to be admitted contrary to this ordinance, as
well the Abbess as the Prioress shall be deposed.   We
decree also the name of masters and Priors that have the
ordering of nuns, if they admit any contrary to this form,
nuns shall also be confessed of priests assigned to them
by the Bishops.   Other clerks or lay shall not have often
recourse to the cloister of nuns without reasonable cause.

CHAPTER VII.

Quoniam inter alia vicia.   Canon of Stephen.

Because the religious specially be assaulted amongst
other vices with the sweetness of their mouths, we decree
that neither monks, neither canons regular presume to
give themselves to eating or drinking but in their houses
appointed, but, if they thirst, let them ask leave according
to their rules, and then go in to their refectory, and so
help their necessity that they follow not their voluptuous-
ness : from this general rule we except all sick and them
that be in the service of prelates.   Furthermore we decree
(statuimus) that, when for weakness or any other just
cause, the monks tarry by themselves in the misericorde
they have always with them at the least two oldermen or
seniors which may refrain and keep down with due correction the lightness of other, and also testify how
misericordly they have used themselves : the same we
will to be kept amongst canons regular and nuns.

CHAPTER VIII.

Sanctimoniales plurimae in vagationis vicis.
Canon of John Peccham.

Any holy nuns, delighting in the vice of wandering by
the example of wandering *Dina*,[a] doth continually fall
into the slander of like corruption, or rather more pernicious : for the which jeopardy we providing, more
desirous to see to their health than to please their vain

[a] Daughter of Jacob. Gen. 34.

desires, do forbid *(inhibemus)* under pain of excommunication, that none of them, either sole or with a
fellow, presume to tarry with their parents or kin, be
they never so nigh, or with strangers of howsoever great
name of dignity or religion they be, above three natural
days for the cause of recreation, neither for any other
necessary cause or occasion (sickness only except) above
six days, except it please the Bishop of that place sometime otherwise upon a cause necessary, whose conscience
we load against that fearful day in this behalf. This
ordinance we stretch not to them that are compelled to
gather without for the things necessary while they go a
begging.

TITULUS 20.

Of Religious Houses.

CHAPTER I.

Plures invenimus.   Canon of John Peccham.

We find many religious houses of the order of
S. Augustine which once did cleave to their mother
Churches of the parts beyond the seas, but now, yea and
long time since, be known to be divided from them
through the occasion of certain ceremonies received by
the said mother houses, by the which ceremonies they
differ from other houses of the same order within the
Province of Canterbury. And therefore they come not
together with other places in their general chapters kept
every third year according to the general council. And
because it is a filthy and uncomely part that agreeth not
with the whole we ordain *(statuimus)* that henceforth all
such houses (the observing of their ceremonies always
saved) be specially admonished by the Bishops of the
places to come together with other canons in the general
chapter, to entreat commonly of the rule and reformation
of their order, or else that they appoint a general chapter
amongst themselves from the other, if there be any

notable diversity betwixt them concerning the very substance of their religion : if not let them be compelled hereto by ecclesiastical censures.

CHAPTER II.

Quoniam religionum.   Canon of Edmund.

Inasmuch as great diversity of religions engendereth great confusion in the Church of God, we command that they which will found of new a hospital or monastery receive of the ordinary of the place the ordinances and rules after the which they may live religiously in order, moreover we straitly command that neither men, neither women, be shut up in any place without special licence of the Diocesan, the place, the manners, the quality of the persons diligently considered : and also wherewith they shall be found moreover no secular persons shall sojourn in their houses without an honest cause and a manifest.

TITULUS 21.

Of the Title of Patronage.

CHAPTER I.

Cum secundum apostolum et infra.   Canon of Stephen.

This thing we judge worthy to be added *(duximus adjungendum)*, that, if two be presented to one Church, the custody shall be committed to neither of them while the cause hangeth, but if the title of giving such benefice according to the authority of the Council be devolved to the Bishop when two patrons strive, whereof either presenteth his clerk, for so much as there ought no prejudice through the Bishop's gift to be engendered to the patron that shall afterward obtain and win the patronage, we decree that the Bishop give that Church for that time to neither of them that be presented unless it be by the consent of both patrons, lest any prejudice in the world should seem to rise to the one of the patrons which perchance afterwards shall overcome.

CHAPTER II.

Si aliquo evincente.   Canon of Boniface.

When one obtaineth in the King's law the title of
patronage against another, and the King writeth unto the
Bishop, or another unto whom institution appertaineth,
to admit him that is presented by him that hath recovered,
if the benefice be void, lest injury be done to the patron
let him that is presented be freely admitted, if no
canonical impediment let, but, if the benefice be not void,
the prelate for his excuse shall shew unto the King or
his justices that because such benefice be not void he
cannot fulfil the King's commandment : notwithstanding
it shall be lawful to the patron to present the possessor
again that by that means the title of the patron that hath
obtained may be declared in time after.

CHAPTER III.

Per nostram provinciam et infra.

Canon of John Peccham.

We decree *(statuimus)* and for ever ordain that no
dean or any other prelate, except Bishops, whose authority
is not refrained by this ordinance, shall make inquisition
concerning the matter and cause of him that is presented
to a benefice, but in a full chapter of that place, the possessioner of the benefice being lawfully called, and having
so much space that he may seek at the counsel of wisemen
and provide sufficient remedy for the defence of his state
and title, whatsoever be attempted hereafter against this
our ordinance we decree *(decernimus)* it not to hold :
condemning nevertheless, by authority of this present
council, such dean or prelate to make satisfaction for all
damages and losses, that the said possessioner hath
suffered by him or them that hath so privily enquired, and
also excluding him that hath so ambitiously laboured
from such office for ever, and suspending him from the
apperning of any other benefice by the space of three
years.

TITULUS 22.

Of Taxes and Proxies.

CHAPTER I.

Ut Singula Ecclesiastica Officia.   Canon of Stephen.

That all and every ecclesiastical office may well proceed in the Church of God, we decree *(statuimus)* that Archdeacons be not grievous unto the Churches subjected unto them, forbidding them straitly to pass the number of waiters[20] assigned in the general council, but let them receive their proxy due in the name of their visitation, and presume not to bid strangers to go with them thereunto : notwithstanding, if for the Archdeacon's honour the parsons of Churches will bid any, we will in nowise forbid them : but the Archdeacons themselves shall bid none, lest perchance they that be not grievous in themselves should be grievous in their guests : wherefore, that necessity and occasion of bidding may be taken away, we forbid Archdeacons to keep chapter the day of their visitation at the Church where they visit, except it chance the Church to be in borough or city, moreover we straitly command Archdeacons that in nowise they take procurations without a reasonable cause, but only for that day upon the which they visit personally the Church that giveth the procurations, or presume totally extort any redemption for visiting.

CHAPTER II.

Ut Archidiaconi et infra.   Canon of Stephen.

We straitly forbid all Archdeacons, deans and officials that they presume not to exercise or require by themselves, or by other, any exactions or tallages of their subjects.

CHAPTER III.

Item contra gravamina.   Canon of Boniface.

We also intending a remedy against the griefs and excesses which (as we be informed), be laid upon the subjects by the Archdeacons and Deans apparitors, we ordain *(statuimus)* that, when it shall happen them as they go to do their executions, or other necessaries, to enter into the houses of parsons, vicars, or chaplains, or other priests, or clerks, or religious persons, they require nothing of them under the name of procurations or other service, but receiving with thanksgiving that which is set before them let them be content: neither shall they make such executions of their commandments by messengers and undersumners but by themselves. And such apparitors as do contrary to this and be grievous or injurious unto the subjects of their lords shall be punished, and shall be bound to restore double to them that be grieved.

CHAPTER IV.

Saeva et miserabilis.   Canon of John Stratford.

Cruel and miserable covetousness hath invented and brought to pass that great exactions oftentimes be made for the letters of institutions of clerks that be admitted unto ecclesiastical benefices: likewise for the letters of orders for the labour of writing and sealing, although the canons forbid it, saying that as it becometh not a Bishop to sell the laying on of his hands, so becometh it not the minister to sell his pension: likewise the clerks of Archdeacons and of their officials and of other refuseth to deliver to them that be presented letters certificatory of the inquisition made upon the vacation of benefices, except they have first an excessive sum of money for the writing, we therefore, willing to put away this abuse, by deliberation of this present council make this order *(duximus ordinandum)* that the said clerks shall not receive by themselves or by other for the writing of letters of inquisitions, of institutions or collations, and commissions to induct, or for certificatories of the same, above twelve pence, and for the letters of any holy orders above six pence. In other things the ordinaries ought to set a stipend to their servants wherewith they ought to be content, but for the sealing of such letters we will nothing to be required, neither paid, of clerks ornated with low or high orders, or any thing to be given for their coming or admission unto the marshals or porters or barbers or doorkeepers, lest, through any cloak or colour, the payment made for the sealing of letters, or for their said coming in, be turned into damnable lucre. And lest any rashness or lightness which violateth this remedy provided should pass unpunished, if contrary to the premises any thing be received we command *(praecipi-mus)* double to be yielded within a month, or else clerks beneficed, which defer to restore double that is unjustly received, know themselves to be suspended from office and benefice : and clerks not beneficed and laymen to be forbid Church entry, until they have made competent satisfaction of the said double to them that paid it unto them.

CHAPTER V.

Quamvis lex naturae et infra. Canon of John Stratford.

By authority of this present council we inhibit that none presume to receive of any Church procurations to be paid by reason of visitation, except he do his office of visitation diligently to the same Church, serving person-ally and looking upon with effect such things as ought to be searched and looked upon. And if any will visit many Churches upon one day, let him be content with one procuration in victual or in money, unto the which pro-curation every Church upon one day so visited shall bear proportionably his part, and if the said visitor have stood at the cost of the parson or vicar visited the night before the visitation, or at the dinner of visitation, and will nevertheless his procuration in money, he shall account the said costs and make allowance for the same in the said procuration or otherwise recompense the same, so that he presume in no wise to exact or receive the said costs above and over the accustomed procuration in money, or any more in money than doth remain after such costs be once

deducted. If any there be that otherwise do, know he
himself to be suspended from Church entry, until he hath
restored that which he hath unjustly received: and
because many Archdeacons and other ordinaries endued
with the prerogative and pre-eminence of honour or of
nobility of stock, when they go in their visitations do pass
the number of servants appointed in the canons, so that
they which pay proxies be ever charged against reason in
victual more than the proxies paid in money was wont to
be.[21] Therefore we leave it in the choice of them that be
visited, whether they will give proxies in money as they
were wont, or else find them victuals. And moreover if
the Church visited have chapels depending on her, we
ordain *(statuimus)* that for the visiting of such Church
and her chapels the Archdeacons and other ordinaries
visiting shall be contented with that procuration which
was wont to be given for one Church in that diocese,
under pain of suspension from office and benefice, into
which they shall run in the deed doing until they have
paid unto the Cathedral Church the double of that which
they have received above one such procuration. Also
because Archdeacons and other ordinaries in their visitations, when they find faults, as well in the Churches as in
the ornaments, and in the closing of churchyards, and in
mansion places, command them to be repaid under pain
pecuniary, and then from extortion get from them that
disobey the said penalty, wherewith the said faults might
be well mended, making their own purses fat wickedly
with the losses of the poor people, in these days (contrary
to the old manner) oppressed. Therefore lest any occasion
through such penal exactions should be ministered to
malice or grudge against Archdeacons and other ordinaries and their ministers, for it becometh not men of the
Church to yane[a] for unhonest and penal lucre or to be
made rich therewith, we decree *(statuimus)* that such
penalties as oft as they be required shall be converted
into the repaying of such faults as be found, under pain
of suspension from their office, wherein we decree them

[a] =yawn, *adhelare.*

to run in so doing that receive the said penalties to themselves contrary to the premises, until such time as they restore with effect that which they have taken, to the reparation of the said faults.

CHAPTER VI.

Item licet quis purgari et infra.
Canon of John Stratford.

Knowing manifestly the abuse of Archdeacons and their officials and of other ordinaries, which do exact of priests that will celebrate within their jurisdictions, before they will suffer them so to do, a great and excessive quantity of money, changing the liberality of priests which were wont to give to the clerks for registering their names one penny into a fee of six pence or thereabout, we therefore decree *(statuimus)* that henceforth the said Archdeacons and other ordinaries or their ministers be not so bold as to receive of the said priests for registering their names, in their first admission to celebrate, above a penny under pain of suspension from celebrating divine service and Church entry, wherein they that do the contrary shall incur, until they have paid the double of that they have received unto the fabric of the Cathedral Church of that place.

CHAPTER VII.

Cum apparitorum et infra.   Canon of John Stratford.

By consent of this present council we ordain *(statuimus)* that every one of our suffragans have one apparitor only, an horseman for their diocese: the Archdeacons of our province for every deanery of their archdeaconry to have one summoner only, not on horseback but on foot going, which shall not tarry with parsons or vicars at their cost above one night and one day every quarter of the year, except they be specially desired by them to tarry; neither yet shall they make any manner gatherings in general chapters, either of money, either of wool, either

K

of lambs, or of any other things : notwithstanding they may receive with thanksgiving such things as be freely given them : but if many be deputed contrary to this, or any deputed be found rather to violate and break the premises, they that have deputed them shall be suspended for their doing from office and benefice, until they have removed such deputies, whom we also suspend for ever from the office of apparitors for that deed doing.

TITULUS 23.

Of celebrating of Masses.

CHAPTER I.

Ad excitandos.   Canon of Stephen.

That the pure hearts of them which labour, in the vineyard of the Lord of strength and power, may be stirred up to receive according to their labour the penny of the true reward, we decree *(decernimus)* that the work of God be not negligently done, specially seeing it is decreed and commanded in the general Council that divine service both by day and night shall be done (according as God hath given it) diligently and devoutly.

Also all manner of Sacraments of the Church and specially of Baptism and of the Altar shall be celebrated and ministered with high devotioñ likewise as God hath inspired.

The words also of the Canon shall be plainly spoken and whole, specially in the Sacraments of the Body and Blood of Christ : also if the priest, after he have received the Lord's Body and Blood, must celebrate again the same day, let him not receive the wine that is poured into the chalice or upon his fingers.

We have also decreed straitly forbidding any priest to celebrate twice in one day, except Christmas Day and Easter Day, or, in the funerals of the dead, the same day that the body is present to be buried, and then the first Mass shall be of the day and the latter for the dead.

Chapter II.

Sacerdotes caveant. Canon of John Peccham.

Let the priests beware that they bind not themselves to the singing of private or peculiar Masses, whereby they may the less serve the Church committed unto them, as they be bound with canonical service.

Neither let any take upon him to sing annuals, except he sing daily for the dead, or cause another specially to sing : moreover none shall receive more annuals to be sung than he hath fellow-priests, except he which procureth suffrages to be done for the dead expressly consent the memory of the dead to be coupled in Mass with another : for let no priest think that he by saying one Mass can satisfy for two, for the which he hath promised specially to sing for everyone by himself, although the canons say that there is no less received, when one Mass is said for many dead, than if a Mass were said for everyone by himself : for if it is spoken of Masses that be said with troubled and combered heart, God forbid that it should be thought of any Catholic man one Mass devoutly said to stretch as far and profit as much a thousand men, for the which perchance it is said, as a thousand Masses said for them with like devotion. For although the sacrifice which is Christ be of infinite virtue, yet He worketh not in the Sacrament or sacrifice the high fulness of His greatness (for, if He did, we needed not to sing for one dead but one Mass) : for God doth work in such mysteries under a certain distribution of His fulness, which He hath knit unto them with a law that cannot be expressed. But as concerning them that have received stipend to celebrate annuals and anniversaries, and of evil mind or negligence do not their duty as they be bound, we monish them that they supply the things omitted and make full satisfaction in time to come. And when soever they it do not, let them give to the poor such fruits as they have received for their souls that give it unto them, or, if they neglect willingly both these things, let them be sharply punished of their ordinaries as deceivers of the Faithful.

CHAPTER III.

Sanctum et salubre et infra.   Canon of John Peccham.

We ordain *(statuimus)* that for every Bishop of the diocese of Canterbury that departeth, the residue of his fellow brethren living shall sing solemn service for the dead, not only in every their chapels, but also whensoever, after the death of one or many Bishops, they come shortly together in counsel or otherwise for the Church profit commanding : moreover and firmly enjoining in virtue of obedience, that all priests, as well secular as religious, as soon as the truth of his death is opened unto them, say every one a Mass for the soul of their diocesan to be purged from the spots of sin. We moreover desire all priests, religious exempt and also secular if any such be, that they will vouchsafe favourably to receive this ordinance, the privileges of their exemption in all other things saved, or at the least make this ordinance of their own authority to be observed and kept, letting them to wit that we shall be glad and thankful for their gentle minds and shall be sorry if we find any unkind.

CHAPTER IV.

Altissimus et infra.   Canon of John Peccham.

At the lifting up of Christ's Body let the bells be rung at the least of the one side[a] that the common people which may not daily hear Mass, wheresoever they be either in the fields or in their houses, may kneel down and receive the indulgencies granted of many Bishops, we also ordain *(statuimus)* that every priest, having no canonical excuse, sing[b] once every week at the least : moreover let the parish priests diligently take heed that they minister not Christ's Body to any person except it first appear unto them, either by witness, either by faithful tokens, that he is confessed : and the whole charge of such certifying we put to his oath that receiveth, who ought to seek those things that be necessary to his own health :

[a] i.e. "chimed."

also none shall give rights to another priest's parishen without evident licence, which ordinance we intend not to stretch to men that journey or that be in jeopardy, neither to let the cause of necessity.

Chapter V.

Quam sit inhonestum et infra.

Canon of John Stratford.

By the assent of our brethren and of the whole council we decree *(decernimus)* that whosoever hereafter sing Mass, in oratories, chapels, or houses not consecrate, or in any place not dedicate, their Diocesan's licence not obtained contrary to the prohibitions of the canons, that he in so doing shall be suspended from celebrating divine service for one month's space, we also decree, that all such manner of licence, to celebrate in places not consecrate, granted by the Bishops of our province and hereafter to be granted to any other persons than great or noble men, which continue in places that be far from the Parish Churches, or be notably weak or diseased, shall be void and of none effect : nevertheless we intend not by this to derogate prelates and parsons and canons of Cathedral Churches and religious, but that they may lawfully celebrate in their oratories builded of old, or cause to be celebrated as it hath been used; moreover we will not that these priests which shall happen to celebrate in the oratories or chapels of Kings or Queens of England, or for any their children, which chapels be now or hereafter, shall be edified to be bound with the aforesaid pain.

Chapter VI.

Praecipimus ne consecretur.   Canon of Richard.

We command *(praecipimus)* that the Eucharist be not consecrated but in a chalice of gold or silver, and that no Bishop after this time hallow any of tin or lead.

CHAPTER VII.

In celebratione missae.   Canon of Edmund.

When the priest at Mass-time will give peace, let him
not put the holy Host into his mouth, for he ought
not to touch it with his mouth before the receipt thereof,
but if he take it from the paten as some do, let the paten
as well as the chalice after Mass be rinsed with water : if
he take it not from the covering, the chalice only shall be
rinsed : let the priest have also nigh hand the Altar a
clean cloth, hanging within another cloth and honestly
and commonly covered round about, wherewith he may
wipe his fingers and his lips, after the receiving of the
wholesome sacrament.

CHAPTER VIII.

Linteamina.   Canon of Walter.

Let the corporals palls and other Altar cloths be whole
and clean, and let them be oftentimes washed by persons
deputed to the same in the canons, for the reverence and
presence of our Saviour and of all the company of heaven,
which no doubt were present at the doing of the Sacrament and also when it was done.

Let also the words of the canon, those specially that
appertain to the holy Sacrament be pronounced full and
whole with high devotion of heart, but yet let not the
priest be so slow in the premises that he make the hearers
weary and so rob his service from fatness of devotion, for
the flies that die do corrupt the sweetness of the ointment,
that is to say the fatness of devotion.

Let moreover no parish priest take upon him to celebrate before he hath said matins and prime and the third
of the day, also no clerk shall be permitted to minister at
the altar except he have a surplus upon him.

And at Mass-time let two candles or one at the least
be lighted.

We forbid also, that no priest fallen into deadly sin
presume to come at the altar to sing Mass before he be

confessed, neither let him think, as some do that err, that mortal sins be washed away by general confession.

Chapter IX.

Presbyteri stipendiarii. Canon of Robert Winchelsea.

Stipendiary priests and other priests that sing[6] within our province, whether they find themselves or be found by other, shall not receive offerings, portions, profits, mass-pence, trentailes, or any manner certainty, specially offerings for the corse present, without licence obtained of the parsons or vicars of the Churches where they serve : neither in any wise shall translate thence these things in prejudice of the parsons or vicars of the said Churches, or in their prejudice that be in their steads, lest they fall into the sentence of the great excommunication promulgated in that behalf. We also decree *(decernimus)* that such priests, serving within our province, be present in the chancel at Matins, at Evensong and other divine service in due hours, wearing surplices which they shall buy at their own cost. And shall not be in the body of the Church or the Churchyard or in the fields.

And if they be corrected for these things by their rulers, let them not disdain, and set up their bristles against them, neither provoke any to support or defend them, but let them be enjoined in virtue of obedience, that they be present at the aforesaid times, reading and singing in psalms. And the said priests shall begin and end their Masses upon the Sundays and holy days, and when the body of any dead is present, after the gospel of high Mass and not before, without licence of the parson or vicar or the ruler asked and obtained.

Chapter X.

Effrenata et infra. Canon of Simon Islepe.

By the counsel and assent of our brethren we decree and ordain *(statuimus et ordinamus)* that chaplains, whatsoever they be not beneficed, specially they which

be meet to serve a cure, shall leave all private and secular
service, and shall serve a parish Church or chapel thereunto belonging for competent stipend, whensoever they
shall be required by the diocesan or any ordinary judge
competent in that behalf, under pain of suspension from
their office : in the which they shall run if when they be
required as aforesaid they effectually within twenty days
space obey not, so there be no lawful impediment to let
them.

CHAPTER XI.

Effrenata et infra.   Canon of Simon Sudbury.

Although Lord Simon Islip of happy memory, late
Archbishop of Canterbury, our predecessor, by the counsel
and assent of his brethren in his lifetime, did statute and
ordain that chaplains celebrating annuals, and other not
intending the cure of souls, shall be contented with the
sum of five marks, and they that served parish Churches,
chapels, or cures to them appertaining, with the sum of
six marks for their yearly stipends, decreeing the pain of
suspension from office against them that obey not, nevertheless we, looking upon the quality of times, by the
counsel and assent of our brethren and suffragans, decree
(statuimus) that whosoever shall celebrate annuals for
souls of the dead, within our diocese or the province of
Canterbury, shall be contented with seven marks, or their
board and three marks, and other that serve cures with
eight marks, or their board and four marks yearly : and
no manner wise to receive above, except the diocesan of
the place first otherwise appoint them to be ordered that
shall serve cures. If any clerk dare break this our constitution, either in giving, either in receiving, he shall fall
into the sentence of excommunication in so doing, from
the which he cannot be rid but by the diocesan of that
place in the which he hath trespassed. And whosoever
break this our present statute, after publication made
thereof according to the canons, we will them to be
wrapped and bound in all sentences contained in the same.

TITULUS 24.

Of Baptism and the effect thereof.

CHAPTER I.

Canon of Edmund.

In every Church where they baptise let there be a font of stone, or of other convenient matter, and let it be commonly covered and reverently kept, and let it not be turned into any other use. Also let not the water wherein a child hath been baptised be kept in the font above seven days.

And if it fortune a child to be baptised at home of the lay in case of necessity, let the water for the reverence of baptism either be poured into the fire or be brought to the Church to be poured into the font, and let the vessel be burned or deputed to the Church use. The priest also shall diligently ask the lay what he said when the child was baptised in necessity, and also what he did. And if, after diligent inquisition made, he truly find that the lay hath baptised distinctly and in form of the Church, whether it were in Latin in English or in French, he shall allow that is done : if not, let him baptise the child as it ought to be according to the form of the Church.

To receive the child from the font, there shall not be past three at the most, in the baptism of the male two men and one woman, in the baptism of the female two women and one man, for whatsoever be more it is of evil.

As appertaining to Baptism and penance, we command that deacons presume not to give penance or to baptise but in such cases as the priest cannot, or is absent, or through foolishness or indiscreetness will not, and death is at hand to the child or the sick : but if the child be baptised of the lay let the things that go before and follow the plunging be fulfilled or supplied of the priest.

CHAPTER II.

Circa sacramentum.   Canon of John Peccham.

About the Sacrament of Baptism we find some to have erred, for although it be granted to the lay, both men and

women, if the younglings be in jeopardy in the article of
necessity to baptise them, and such manner of baptism to
be sufficient if due form be kept, neither ought they to be
rebaptised, that be so baptised : notwithstanding some
foolish priests do baptise again the young ones so baptised, not without the injury of the sacrament : which
thing hereafter to be done we utterly forbid, but let the
adjurations against the devil and the instructions of the
faith be said over the baptised, for the reverence of the
Church that hath so decreed.

The form of the Sacrament in the common tongue,
standeth not only in the signs, but also in the order of the
selfsame words with which the sacrament is instituted of
God, whereby Christ the Lord hath given regenerative
power unto these words ordered as they be in the Latin
tongue : therefore let it thus be spoken of them that do
baptise, *I christen thee in the name of the Father and of
the Son and of the Holy Ghost,* or otherwise in the mother
tongue after the country custom, or in French thus, *Je te
baptize au nom du père, et du filz, et du saynct esperit.*

But if the priest probably doubt whether the little one
be baptised in due form or not, let him say (observing the
manner of the decretal with adjurations and instructions)
*if thou be baptised I do not baptise thee again, if thou be
not yet baptised I baptise thee in the name of the Father,
and of the Son, and of the Holy Ghost.*

Let the priests also take heed that they suffer not nyse
and wanton names to be given to the youngles when they
be baptised specially of the women kind, which names
spoken sound to wantons, and, if the contrary be done,
let it be redressed by the Bishops that confirm them.

CHAPTER III.

Quod in constitutione.   Canon of John Peccham.

Whereas in the constitution of Othobone it is provided
that children which must be baptised shall be kept unto
the general baptism of Easter and Pentecost, for the
reverence of the statute which seemeth hitherto to be

neglected, we have judged it thus to be declared *(duximus declarandum)* that children delivered from the mothers' wombs in the eight days before Easter and so many before Pentecost, if they may without jeopardy, shall be reserved and kept unto these times to be baptised, so that in the mean time betwixt the birth of the children and perfect baptism they receive information with adjurations and other service before baptism, and only the plunging to be left for the days of baptism. Also other that be born other seasons of the year, partly for jeopardy of death, which cometh suddenly often to children, and partly for the simplicity of their parents which be ready to err about the form of baptism, let them be baptised after the old custom without any note of offence, either incontinent when they be born, either afterwards as it shall please the parents.

TITULUS 25.

Of the keeping of the Host, of the Chrism and of the Holy Oil.

CHAPTER I.

Fontes baptismales.   Canon of Edmund.

The baptising font must be kept close under lock, for fear of witchcrafts: likewise the Chrism and the Holy Oil shall be kept under key: and if he to whom the custody appertaineth negligently leave them, he shall be suspended from his office three months, and if through his negligence any mischance happen he shall be sorer punished.

CHAPTER II.

Dignissimum eucharistiae.   Canon of John Peccham.

We command *(praecipimus)* the most worthy sacrament of the Altar from henceforth so to be kept, that in every parish Church there be a tabernacle, with a closing commonly made, and worthily as the greatness of the cure and the ability of the Church may bear, in the which the Lord's Body may be collocate, and in nowise shall it be put in a purse or bag for fear of breaking, but in a fair pyx garnished within with the purest linen, so that, without jeopardy of breaking, it may lightly be taken out and put in, which honourable sacrament we command every Sunday to be renewed. And the priest which is negligent in keeping of the sacrament shall be punished after the rule of the general council, and sharplier if he continue in negligence.

TITULUS 26.

Of reliques and honouring of Saints.

CHAPTER I.

Ad exemplum.   Canon of Stephen.

According to the example of Solomon which hath appropriate to the service of God all the vessels of the temple made of pure gold, we ordain *(statuimus)* that every Church have a chalice of silver, with other vessels according : a clean corporis and white of convenient largeness : and all the old corporals which be not meet for the altar forasmuch as they be consecrated, let them be laid up in the place of reliques or else be burned in the presence of the Archdeacon.

CHAPTER II.

Dignissimum et infra.   Canon of John Peccham.

We ordain *(statuimus)* the sacrament of the Altar to be borne to the sick with due reverence, the priest having upon him at the least a surplice with a stole and light borne before him in a lantern with a bell, that the people may be stirred up to due reverence, which must be informed, by the priest's wisdom, to kneel down, and the least humble to pray unto and honour the same, wheresoever it happen the king of Glory hidden in bread to be borne. And for this thing let Archdeacons and other visitors be diligent and careful, unto the remission of their trespasses. And whom they shall find negligent herein, let them be sharply punished.

TITULUS 27.

Of the building of Churches.

CHAPTER I.

Si rector ecclesiae.   Canon of Edmund.

If the parson of any Church depart, leaving the Church housing down or ruinous, such portion shall be deducted out of his ecclesiastical goods as shall suffice to repair them and to supply other faults of the Church. The same thing we decree *(statuimus)* about vicars which have all the provents of the Church paying a little pension, for, seeing they be bound to the premises, such sufficient portion deducted may and ought to be accounted amongst debts: nevertheless reasonable consideration must be taken according to the power of the Church, when this portion shall be deducted.

CHAPTER II.

Ut parochiani.   Canon of Robert Winchelsea.

That the parishioners of all Churches of our province of Canterbury may be certain of all defaults that appertain to their charges, lest betwixt them and their parsons any doubt should rise in succession of time, we will and command *(praecipimus)* that hereafter they find all these things hereunder specified: a legend, an antiphonary, a graile, a psalter, a book of sequences, an ordinal, a massbook, a manual, a chalice, a principal vestment with his chasuble and alb, a cope for the choir with all appendants, a pall for the high altar with three towels, three surplices, one rochet, a cross for procession, and another to serve for the dead, a censer, a lantern, and a little bell to go before the Body of Christ in the visiting of sick, an honest pyx for the said body, a veil for the Lent season,

banners for Rogation, dayes bells with their cords, a bier
for the dead, a vessel for holy water, a pax, a candle-
stick for the paschal, a font with his lock, images in the
Church, the principal image in the Chancel, the closing of
the Church yard, the repairing of the body of the Church
both within and without, as well in images as in glass
windows, the repairing of books and vestments whensoever it happen them to need.   As for *all* other things that
be not here expressed, as well concerning the *reparation
of the chancel*[22] as other things they must be repaired
throughout by the parsons or vicars or other to whom it
appertaineth after the diversity of approbated customs of
the places.

CHAPTER III.

Statuimus quod nulla inquisitio.
Canon of Simon Mepham.

We ordain *(statuimus)* that no inquisition that shall
hereafter be made, upon the faults of the housing or other
things appertaining to a benefice, shall prevail in prejudice
of another, except it be made by faithful men sworn in
form of law, he also being first called whose interest it is.
And then the whole and true estimation of all faults
which be found in the houses, or in other things appertaining to the said benefice, whether they be found by
inquisition or by way of composition, the diocesan of that
place shall cause the same to be bestowed in reparation of
the said faults, within a competent season to be set and
appointed by his discretion.

CHAPTER IV.

Licet parochiani et infra.   Canon of John Stratford.

By approbation of this present Council we ordain
(duximus statuendum) that as well religious persons as
other which do obtain, or here after shall obtain, in any
parish of our province, possessions, lands or reddites[23]
which be not of the glebe or dowry of Churches that

must be repaired, wheresoever the said persons dwell,
whether within that parish or elsewhere, shall bear their
parts unto all manner of charges that appertain by law
or custom to the said parishes or the Church or ornaments
of the same, according to the quality of their said possessions or reddites, considered and compared to other of
the parish : whereunto they shall be compelled by the
ordinaries of that place, if it so require with ecclesiastical
censures and other remedies of the law.

TITULUS 28.

Of the Church's Liberties.[24]

CHAPTER I.

Porro et infra.   Canon of Boniface.

We ordain that such as will not suffer feod to be ministered unto them that flee to the Church's liberties, shall
be punished after the ordinaries discretion by ecclesiastical censures. And whosoever pluck or draw them
from the Church or Churchyard, or after their abjuration
from the high way, or, after they be so drawn, flay them
being under protection of the Church, shall be punished
by all penalties of sacrilege, and the one penalty shall not
consume the other : moreover there shall none be set to
watch or keep them that take Church or Churchyard if
there be : as well the keepers as they that set them shall
be driven away in form of law, by the sentence of excommunication. The Church also shall defend them only
which the canons command to be defended.

CHAPTER II.

Ut invadentibus.   Canon of Boniface.

That they which invade the Church's goods and break
the Church's liberties may be withstood, we decree
(duximus statuendum) that such malefactors be denounced by the ordinaries of the places for sacrilege and
excommunicate persons : and if they continue in their

malice by one month, then the lands and places where they abide shall be interdicted : and neither sentence shall be released until they have made sufficient amends for the damages and injuries. And if any, not regarding the honour of God, spoil the Church of her possessions or her liberties, let them be under the said penalties, and let the sentence of excommunication be solemnly pronounced against them in form of law, until full restitution and worthy satisfaction be made. And if the said committers of sacrilege cause the judges or prelates for this cause to be attached and distrained, as well they as the distrainers shall be punished by all penalties made against attachers and distrainers.

Chapter III.

Contingit aliquando.   Canon of Boniface.

When the King hath the custody of Cathedral or conventual Churches, although according to the Charter of Liberties granted to the Church by him and his predecessors he ought to receive only certain profits and certain services, and that without the distraining of men and destruction of things, it chanceth nevertheless that his bailees, through immoderate tallages and exactions, doth both violently take away the Church's tenants' goods in time of vacation, and also destroyeth parks, woods, store pools, houses, and scattereth the goods abroad : they evil entreat the power and stretch their hands not only to those things which they were wont to obtain by reason of custody, but also unto the goods of them that remain in life that is, to wit that blade and store and such other wherewith the Chapter and Convent ought to be sustained : yea, and presume to take other things, likewise which by reason of barony can in no wise appertain unto him, as tithes and oblations belonging and appertaining to Churches appropriate unto Bishoprics and monasteries and other like things.

Therefore to withstand this evil we ordain *(ordinamus)* that as soon as the King's excheters and bailees shall have entered such custody, the prelates which have jurisdictions shall openly and solemnly forbid all the said bailees generally, that under pain of excommunication they attempt no such things. But if they do the contrary, let it be openly declared that they be fallen into the sentence of excommunication decreed against the violators and troublers of the Church's liberties, until they have competent amends for the hurts and injuries. Which sentence if they despise after such denunciation, let process be made against them by interdictions and other penalties ordained against such wrong doers.

And except the King admonished thereof, make competent restitution, or cause the things so taken to be restored, and amend or cause such hurts done by his to be amended, let process be made against him, as it is decreed in other cases touching the King. And the self same things which are before decreed for the King and his ministers we will to be observed in other inferior lords if peradventure the custody come to them.

Chapter IV.

Accidit novitate.   Canon of John Stratford.

Through frowardness risen of late it chanceth that, when the prelates of Churches go about to enquire of the discipline and order of manners and of the faults and transgressions of the subjects, the great men and other secular powers, labouring to let and withstand the duties and offices of the spiritual, doth forbid the lay (such as be their tenants or bond men) the spiritual court that they shall not go or appear out of the place of their lordship before their ordinaries when they be cited, either to receive canonical correction for their faults and excesses, the punishment whereof and correction is known to appertain by law or custom unto the ordinaries, either for the insinuation or probations of testaments or accounts and reckonings upon the administration of the dead's goods or for other testamentary titles : and do also let and cause other wickedly to let and withstand that the

L

premises cannot be exercised by the prelates within the places of their lordships, usurping to themselves jurisdictions in these things : other there are which, when men of the Church that have ecclesiastical jurisdiction do enjoin unto their subjects for their faults and offences penance corporal or pecuniary, and cause them to do the same as it is lawful to the said ordinaries to do, or for their corporal penance enjoined according to the measure of their offences do admit and receive bursall redemption as they justly may, do indict the same ordinaries upon great extortions, and so indicted do attach them, and imprison them and compel them to make answer to them upon these things in the secular court, and there they procure and cause unjustly at their own pleasured pecuniary mulcts and mercements to be set upon them by the said occasion : and moreover oftentimes many run to go there in great companies and with much clamour and noise come unto the ecclesiastical courts, and very grievously fear the judges and suitors and other that have ought there to do, whereby ecclesiastical jurisdiction is confounded and the office of prelates is opprobriously suspended and wickedly let : and men that lightly fall into vice, while there is no punishment to keep down transgressors, doth promise and nourish to themselves penal impunity, and prepare a smooth and much haunted way unto the crafts and baits of the old enemy. Another sort there is that procureth and causeth many because they move matters and causes against their adversaries in the spiritual court which ought in deed in law or custom there to be entreated, and like wise their advocates that speak for them, and procurators with other ecclesiastical ministers and judges that take cognition of the same matters, to be indicted attached and imprisoned and otherwise to be fatigated divers ways in the secular court. And if any tenants or other run to the spiritual courts for matters or causes which ought by the law or custom there to be handled, and will not cease from thence and take their actions in the temporal courts, for the same causes they oftentimes charge them with great mercements and unjustly vex them with much labours and expenses. And another sort there is that when the Bishops would duly exercise their jurisdictions in Cytes[a] or other places subjected unto them upon such causes as notably appertain to them, or else for the exercising of ecclesiastical jurisdiction, send forth their canonical and lawful commandments and their executions in due manner to be fulfilled, doth stop and let and cause other to stop and let the same unjustly, and presume to take, beat and entreat maliciously and injuriously the messengers that carry such commandments and would do duly just executions. Yea and some temporal lords and their bailees, pretending the goods of them that die intestate to be devolved (although erroneously) to the said lords, make distresses in the same goods so that the ordinaries cannot convert them into the payment of the debts of them that so depart, or into any other holy uses for the soul's health, as it was ordained of old, by the King's consent and the nobles of the realm of England in the derogation of the Church's liberty, and the great impediment and hindrance of the spiritual law and jurisdiction.

Therefore we by deliberation of this present council do pronounce (*pronuntiamus*) all and singular transgressors in the premises or in any part of them, and consenters to the premises or to any part of them, or such as do give counsel help or favour to the same, or do allow and ratify any of the premises done in their causes or names, to be wrapped in the sentence of the great excommunication, whose absolution we reserve specially to the diocesans of the places. And moreover command all such transgressors generally four times in the year openly to be denounced excommunicated in all Parish Churches of our province of Canterbury.

CHAPTER V.

Saeculi principes.   Canon of John Stratford.

Princes of the world which have received power of God be wont to get and obtain that of the obstinate people by

[a] i.e. cities.

the fear of punishment and the sword of their power, which the rulers of the Church could not once fasten in their necks : wherefore honourable antiquity doth inform us that if excommunicate persons arrogantly cast off from them with hard heart the benefit of humility and the desire of reconciling, the King's power called in to help is bound by the due rigour of justice to keep in prison such rebellious. But it happeneth sometime that, when certain persons be excommunicated, and that for manifest offences, and then at the signification of prelates according to the custom of England be taken and cast into prison, the Bishops be commanded by the King's briefs, that if the imprisoned will find surety to obey the law and the commandments of the Church, to deliver them from the prisons where they be : but if the Bishops do it not, as they neither may, neither ought, to do by the law before due satisfaction, another brief is directed to the sheriffs, that they (after such caution of the imprisoned be received) shall deliver them without delay. Moreover, when suggestion is made to the King's Court (although not truly) that such excommunicated are ready to obey the Church's commandments, there be precepts made to the sheriffs that they shall deliver and let go the said excommunicated, no mention made of the parties at whose instance they were excommunicated. And sometime when suggestion is made as before said, that the said imprisoned be excommunicated for such cause as apperteineth not to the spiritual court, then have the sheriffs in commandments that if such be excommunicated and imprisoned for such cause and none other, to cause the Bishops to deliver them shortly. And no credence or faith is given to the processes of the spiritual judges upon such cause of excommunication. And so the excommunicated in the said cases be unjustly delivered at such commandments and precepts, whereby the ecclesiastical judges' office is confounded and made vain, while the lay judges which have not the key and power of knowledge (which they are so straitly bound to follow and obey that the authority of examination, judging and commanding is utterly forbidden them in all such things as appertaineth to the spiritual jurisdiction) go about to cut down another man's corn : and though the wicked company of the excommunicated persons, unjustly as before said delivered, as well the sheriffs and bailees that deliver them as other common and faithful people that keep company with such excommunicated, be pestiferously defiled and their souls loaded with great jeopardy and perils. Against which things we be moved with fervent charity to provide some remedy. And therefore we enact that if any excommunicated in our province and imprisoned do so depart from prison contrary to the liberties and customs of the Church of England they shall be openly denounced accursed unto their greater confusion and shame in places notable, solemnly with ringing of bells and lighting of candles, and shall utterly be forbidden the company of all faithful, and to buy and sell or otherwise to bargain or contract for their own profit. And all that unlawfully company with them shall be sharply punished by the censures of the Church, no regard of persons taken in that behalf.

Chapter VI.

Quia divinis. Canon of John Stratford.

Forasmuch as the lay be forbidden as well by the laws of God as of man to order or dispose the Church's goods, it is manifest therefore that this unjust usurping must be laid aside, whereby certain parishens within our province of Canterbury, either being ignorant what they may do or rather arrogantly passing the bonds limited unto them, do pluck up by the roots and cut down trees and grass which grow in the yards of Churches and chapels at their own pleasures, contrary and beside the will of parsons and vicars and their deputies, applying the same to their own uses or their Churches or some others. And so they boldly commit sacrilege to the jeopardies of their souls. And great contentions, strifes, and evil occasions do rise

almost daily betwixt the rulers of Churches and their
parishens by means thereof, wherefore by authority of
this present Council we decree *(praecipimus)* such bold
despisers of the law to be wrapped in the sentences of the
great excommunication, comprehended as well in the constitution of Othobone, once legate of the See of Rome in
England, as in the Council of Oxford, made against the
violators of the Church's liberties. And whosoever hereafter unlawfully usurp in these things, we command them
to be openly and solemnly declared accursed by the parsons or vicars, which perceive their Churches to be hurt
through the premises. And the said usurpers we decree
to be put from the company of the faithful to their confusion and shame until they offer and make effectual
amends for the premises.

Taken out of the King's answers.

CHAPTER VII.

Sciatis quod cum Dudum et infra.

It pleaseth the King's highness that hereafter no distrains be made, neither in Church feod, neither in the
King's way, neither in the lands wherewith the Churches
have been of old time endued : notwithstanding, in such
possessions as men of the Church have gotten the said
distresses may be made. Also a clerk that fleeth to the
Church for felony, to have liberties thereof affirming
himself to be a clerk, shall not be compelled to abjure the
realm, but, delivering himself of the realm, shall enjoy the
Church's liberty according to the laudable custom of the
realm hitherto used. Also the benefice of the Church's
liberty is likewise given to him that appealeth in due form
as it is to a clerk, which is required by his ordinary (which
text Lyndwood readeth thus). Also the benefice of the
Church's liberty shall be given to a clerk that approacheth
other, as unto him that is required by his ordinary in due
form.

TITULUS 29.

Chapter I.

Cum viris religiosis et infra. Canon of Stephen.

We ordain *(decernimus)* that neither monk, neither canon regular, may take to farm Church, manor, land, or any other thing of his own house : we also straitly forbid the keeping of any manor to be committed to monk or canon regular, which is not always under obedience, lest through his long absence from his monastery or his lewd conversation some slander rise : if the contrary be presumed let it be amended by the superior. Also religious persons may not take that Church to farm, specially after the person's death wherein they claim any right : if they do they shall be punished at the superior's arbitrament.

Chapter II.

Presenti decreto. Canon of Stephen.

By this present ordinance we enact and decree *(statuimus)* that clerks beneficed, or within Holy Orders, shall not be made procurators of lordships, that is to wit, they shall not be stewards or bailees of such offices as by occasion thereof they should be bound to accounts making unto the lay, nor shall exercise secular jurisdictions, specially those that have the judgment of blood annexed to them. And unto this we thought it best to add that the judgment of blood be not kept in holy places as in the Church or Churchyard. And further, by authority of this present council, we straitly inhibit that no clerk having benefice or holy orders presume to write or indite letters for the executing of the pain of blood or to be present where the judgment of blood is kept or exercised : for be it known unto such that they be unworthy of the Church's protection, seeing through them presuming such things slander is engendered in the Church of God.

The End of the Third Book.

THE FOURTH BOOK.

TITULUS 1.

Of Promises and Matrimony.[25]

Matrimonium. Canon of Walter.

Matrimony must be celebrated with honour and reverence as other sacraments be, by day time, in the sight of the people, and not with laughing and sporting and little regard, moreover in the knitting of matrimony the priests always by three Sundays or sundry Feasts must make three proclamations and enquire of the people the freeness of the spouse and spousess: if any priest observe and keep not such proclamations he shall not escape the pain lately in the Council for the same appointed: let the priests also warn and forbid oftentimes that such as will contract matrimony betroweth not themself, but in open place before known and many persons called together for the same purpose.

TITULUS 2.

Of the Marriage of them that be under age.

Ubi non est consensus. Canon of Edmund.

Where as is not the consent of both parties there is no bond of matrimony, therefore such as give to young boys young lasses in their youth do nothing at all except the children after they come to the years of discretion consent thereunto. By authority therefore of this ordinance we forbid that henceforth none be joined or set together, whereof both or the one be not come to the age appointed by the laws and the canons except there be an urgent cause of that such conjunction should be suffered for the goodness of peace.

TITULUS 3.

Of Privy Marriages.

CHAPTER I.

Quia ex contractibus. Canon of Simon Mepham.

Forasmuch as where marriages be made no Banns asked before, many jeopardies have risen to men's souls and manifest it is daily do rise, we command *(praecipimus)* all and every our suffragans that upon certain solemn days when the great multitude of people is present they cause the decretal law *Cum inhibitio &c.*, wherein marriages are forbidden to be made without Banns asking and proclamations making, to be declared and expounded in the vulgar tongue in all parish church of the Diocese, and cause the same law to be firmly kept and observed of all priests : yea though they be not parish priests, punishing them by the pain of suspension from office for three years space that presume to be present at such marriages as be made before the Banns be asked after the accustomed manner, and also correcting them with just punishment that so do marry if there be none impediment. And whatsoever priest, whether he be secular or regular, presume to celebrate the solemnization of matrimony without the parish church, having no special licence of the Bishop of the Diocese thereunto or be present thereat, he shall be suspended from his office for one whole year.

CHAPTER II.

Humana concupiscentia et infra.
Canon of John Stratford.

By authority of this present Council we enact *(statuimus)* and ordain that such as hereafter contract matrimony and cause the same openly to be solemnized, having knowledge of any likely presumption of canonical impediments in that behalf, and likewise priests which hereafter wittingly execute the solemnizing of such marriages as be forbidden betwixt any other than their

own parishioners, except they have obtained a licence of
the Diocesan or of the curate of them that be married.
And moreover such as hereafter cause, either through
violence either fear, privy matrimonies to be solemnized
in churches, oratories, or chapels, or be present at the
solemnization of such foresaid marriages, having knowledge of the premises, shall incur in the deed doing the
sentence of the great excommunication. And we will
that every year four times they be openly denounced excommunicated in common, and shall nevertheless suffer
the pains decreed by the law against them that celebrate
matrimony without Banns asking or otherwise privily.
And forasmuch as the constitution of good memory
Simon Mepham once Archbishop of Canterbury our next
predecessor whose beginning is in Latin *Item quia ex
contractibus &c.* seemeth by the opinion of many in the
end to be doubtful or obscure after the bark or outward
sound of his words, intending to make the same constitution for all times to come certain and without doubt, by
the agreement of this Council we declare the same thus
to be understood, that whatsoever priest, secular or
regular, presume to be present at the solemnization of
matrimony, without it be in a parish church or chapel
having of old time the rights of a parish church appertaining unto it, shall receive in so doing the pain in the
same decreed.

The End of the Fourth Book.

THE FIFTH BOOK.

TITULUS 1.

Of Accusations, Denunciations and Inquisitions.

Sint in quolibet decanatu.   Canon of Edmund.

Let there be in every deanery two or three men, having God before their eyes, which being appointed at the commandment of the Bishop or his officials, may denounce unto them the open and notorious excesses of the prelates and other clerks.

TITULUS 2.

Of Simony.

CHAPTER I.

Firmiter Inhibemus.   Canon of Stephen.

We firmly forbid any to be denied, through the lack of money, sepulture or baptism or any other Sacrament of the Church, and that matrimony be not letted to be made, for if aught have been accustomed to be given through the godly devotion of the faithful, we will that justice therein be ministered to the churches, afterward by the Ordinary of that place as it is expressly decreed in the General Council. We also judge it unmeet that aught hereafter should be required or given for oil and anointing, seeing it is found so often forbidden : if any presume to do contrary hereunto let him be denounced an antheme, that is, with all solemnity accursed.

CHAPTER II.

Praeterea statuimus.   Canon of Stephen.

·Furthermore by assent of this present Council we ordain that none henceforth presume to take from any person by extortion, money, or any other thing, for the receiving of him into any house of religion, insomuch as, if he that entereth must clothe himself through the poverty of the house, there shall be nothing in the world received of him under the pretence of clothing more than the true and just price thereof.

CHAPTER III.

Praeterea venalitatem massarum.   Canon of Edmund.

Furthermore we, straitly forbidding the sale of Masses, do command *(praecipimus)* that no lay or other presume to give or bequeath in their testament any thing for an annual of masses or a trental. And we also forbid any manner paction, true or by any wise cloked, to be made by priests or other mediators. And lest priests should at any time load themself with the superfluous multitude of such annuity of masses, which they cannot fulfil honestly themself, and therefore must have under them other priests hired for a certain price, or else sell them to other to be sung to unload and discharge themself, we that thing hereafter to be done forbid under pain of suspension.

CHAPTER IV.

Nulli liceat ecclesiam.   Canon of Edmund.

It shall moreover be lawful for none to give a church to any other under the name of dowry making, or to receive, by paction or promise, money or other advantage for the presenting of any person : which thing if any do and be thereof convicted or confess it in a judgment, we do enact and make, *(statuimus)* using as well the King's authority as our own, that he shall be deprived for ever of the patronage of that church.

TITULUS 3.

That prelates let not to farm their offices for annual rent.

Ut omnis cupiditatis.   Canon of Stephen.

That all desire and covetousness may be expelled from ministers in the Church of God, we ordain *(statuimus)* that archdeaconries, deaneries and other offices which be mere spiritual shall not be let to farm, but, if there be a certain temporal profit annexed to this office, that may be let to farm by the superior's licence as it is decreed of other benefices : if any dare do contrary to this present statute, whether he be archdeacon or dean, or have any manner such office, and thereof be canonically convicted, he shall be suspended by his Bishop from such office for one year, and another shall be appointed that may in the meantime with discretion occupy his place.

TITULUS 4.

Of Masters and the authority of Teaching.

CHAPTER I.

Reverendissimae synodo et infra.
                    Canon of Thomas Arundel.

Because an old potschard savoureth of that wherewith it was seasoned when it was new, we ordain and decree *(statuimus et ordinamus)* that masters and such as teach children or any other, in sciences *(artibus)* or in grammar instructing them in the first principles, shall in no wise meddle to instruct them in the Catholic Faith, in the Sacrament of the Altar, or other Sacraments of the Church, or in any other divine matter, contrary to the determination of the Church, neither shall interpretate nor declare Holy Scripture in expounding the text, but as it hath been of old time accustomed. They shall not moreover suffer their scholars or disciples to dispute openly or privily of the universal faith or the Sacraments of the

Church : he that doth otherwise shall be grievously punished by the Ordinary of that places as a favourer of
errors and schisms.

CHAPTER II.

Quia insuper nova via.   Canon of Thomas Arundel.

Furthermore, because a new way doth oftener deceive
than an old, we will and ordain *(volumus et ordinamus)*
that no book or treatise newly made by John Wycliffe or
any other in his time or since, or hereafter to be made,
from henceforth be read in schools, halls, hostels or any
other places within our province aforesaid. And that no
manner of doctrine after such books be taught, except
the books be first examined by the University of Oxford
and Cambridge, or at the least by twelve persons of the
same, which the said Universities or the one of them
shall think worthy to be chosen by the laudable discretion
of us or our successors, and so examined, all agreeing in
one, be expressly approved by us or our successors, and in
the name of the University be delivered to the stationaries
to be copied and, after faithful collation made, be sold at
a just price or given : the original afterwards remaining
for ever in some chest of the University : but if any read
such book or treatise in schools or elsewhere as beforesaid, or teach after them contrary to the form before
limited, he shall be punished as a sower of schisms and a
favourer of heresies according to the quality of his fault.

CHAPTER III.

Periculosa res est.   Canon of Thomas Arundel.

It is a very jeopardous thing (witnessing the same
Saint Jerome) to translate the text of Holy Scripture
from one tongue into another, because the same sense
doth not lightly abide throughout in the translations, as
the self same Saint Jerome (although he were inspired)
knowledgeth himself therein oftentime to have erred.
Therefore we enact and ordain *(statuimus)* that none

hereafter translate upon his own authority any manner text of Holy Scripture into the English tongue or any other tongue in manner of a work, book, or treatise. And that no such work, book, or treatise be read openly or privily, in part or in whole, which was made lately in the time of the said John Wycliffe, or since, or hereafter shall be made, under the pain of the great excommunication, until such time as that translation be approved by the Diocesan of that place, or if the thing so require by the Council Provincial. And he that doth contrary to this shall be likewise punished as the favourer of heresy and error.

CHAPTER IV.

Praeterea cum terminis.   Canon of Thomas Arundel.

Furthermore, seeing that He which hath set the bounds and end of all things can not be comprehended with any conclusion of philosophy or any invention of man, and seeing that Saint Augustine hath oftentimes revoked true conclusions which grudged and displeased religious ears, we ordain *(statuimus)* and under obtestation of the divine judgment we specially inhibit, that none of whatsoever degree, state, or condition he be, hold or put forth conclusions or propositions of the Catholic Faith, or words sounding anywise contrary to good manners, otherwise than the doctrine of the faculty do necessary require, whether it be done in schools or out of schools, in disputing or communing, under protestation or without protestation, not though the said conclusions or propositions may be defended by the subtility of words and terms, for Saint Hugh writing of the Sacraments witnesseth that thing oftentimes not to be well understood which is well spoken. And if any other person, after publication of these presents, shall be convicted that he hath wittingly put forth or held such conclusions or propositions, except he be monished amend himself within a month, shall incur in the deed doing the sentence of the great excommunication, by authority of this present ordinance, and shall be

openly denounced for an excommunicated person, until
such time as he openly knowledge his fault in the place
where he put them forth and held them, and openly
preach, at the Ordinary's arbitrament, the true and
catholic meaning of the same conclusion or proposition,
either in one church, either in divers as it shall seem to the
Ordinary expedient.

TITULUS 5.

Of Heretics and Schismatics.

CHAPTER I.

Reverendissimae synodo et infra.

Canon of Thomas Arundel.

We enact, decree and ordain *(statuimus decernimus et
ordinamus)* that no secular or regular which is not
authorised by the law, or otherwise specially privileged,
to preach the word of God shall take upon him the office
or use of preaching the said Word of God, or in any wise
preach to the people or clergy in the Latin tongue, or in
any vulgar tongue, within churches or without, except he
first present himself to the Diocesan of that place where
he intendeth to preach, and of him be examined and, when
he is found apt and meet both in manners and knowledge,
be then sent to preach by the Diocesan unto one certain
parish, or unto many, as it shall seem expedient to the
Ordinary after the quality of the person. And also none
of the foresaid shall presume to preach until it first
appear in due form that he is sent or authorised, so that
he which is authorised by the law shall come in the
manner limited to him in that behalf. And they which
affirm themselves under special privilege shall really
exhibit and show their privilege to the person or vicar of
that place where they preach. And such as pretend to be
sent by the Diocesan of the place shall likewise show the
letters of the Diocesan made for that purpose under his
great seal. The perpetual curate we understand should
be sent by the law to the place and people of his own

cure : notwithstanding, if it happen any such to be suspended or prohibited from such preaching by the Diocesan of that place, or any other superior, for errors or heresies which it is pretended that he hath preached, affirmed or thought, then may he not in any wise meddle with preaching in any place within our Diocese, until that blot be cleansed and washed away at the just arbitrament of him that did suspend or inhibit him, and he lawfully be restored again unto preaching, of which his restitution he shall carry with him letters testimonial in all places where he shall afterwards preach, and shall really exhibit the same in form and manner aforesaid : but the parish priests, or vicars temporal and not perpetual, being not sent in manner before written, may preach in the Churches where they serve those things only, and that plainly and simply with prayers accustomed, which things be expressly contained in the Constitution Provincial beginning *Ignorantia Sacerdotum &c.,* which was well and godly made by John of good memory our predecessor for the supplying of the ignorance of priests, which constitution we will to be had in all churches of our Province of Canterbury within three months after publication of these presents, and to be effectually declared by the priests at times yearly as it doth require.

And lest this wholesome statute might seem to bring hurt by means of exactions of money, or any other difficulty, we will and ordain that the examination of persons of which mention is before made, and the Diocesan's letters for them, be speedily done, all manner difficulty put apart and freely, without exaction of money, by them to whom it appertaineth and belongeth to examine and deliver the said letters : if any presume wittingly to violate or break this our statute (by the which we execute the old law) after publication of the same through his rash preaching, contrary to the manner therein described, shall in so doing incur the sentence of the great excommunication, which absolution by tenour hereof we specially reserve unto us and our successors. But if any preacher do despise this wholesome statute and, not re-

M

garding the sentence of excommunication, do preach of
his own head, again saying, affirming, or obstinately in
word or deed declaring, that the said sentence of excommunication may not be decreed and commanded by the
Church in the persons of her prelates, we will then that
further process be made against them by the superiors of
the places and that the company of all faithful be utterly
forbidden them.

And hereof lawful convicted, except they repent and
abjure according to the accustomed manner of the Church,
they shall be declared for heretics by the Ordinary of that
place.   And thenceforth shall be taken for heretics and
schismatics unto all effect of the law.   And in so doing
shall incur the pains of heresy and schism in the law expressed.

And specially their goods shall be judged forfeit by the
law, and shall be seasoned by them that have interest.
And likewise their favourers, receivers and defenders
shall suffer the same penalty in all things, if they, lawfully monished by their superiors in that behalf, cease not
within a month, and thereof be convicted.

Furthermore the clergy or people, of whatsoever parish
or place within our Province of Canterbury they be, shall
admit none to preach in churches, churchyards, or any
other places, except they first make a proof according to
the aforesaid form of their authorising privilege or send-
ing.   And if they otherwise admit any the church, churchyard, or place where such preaching was, shall be under
church interdicting in the deed doing.   And so shall continue interdicted until they which so admitted or suffered
any to preach duly amend themself and obtain of their
Diocesan or other superior ordinary the same interdiction
to be relieved in due form of the law.   Moreover, like as
a good husband casteth his corn into the ground that is
ordered therefore, that it may bring more fruit, we will
and command that the preacher of the Word of God,
coming after the manner before noted, behave himself
honestly in preaching to the clergy or the people according
to the matter intended, casting his seed abroad as his

audience shall require : that is to say, he shall preach to
the clergy of the vices that rise amongst them and unto
the lay of their sin which is commonly used amongst
them, and not contrary wise, for if he do otherwise preach
he shall be canonically and sharply punished by the
Ordinary of that place according to the quality of his
fault.

Chapter II.

Item quia turpis est pars.   Canon of Thomas Arundel.

For so much as that part is foul which agreeth not with
the whole body, we ordain and decree *(decernimus et
ordinamus)* that no preacher of the Word of God, or any
other person, may teach, preach, or observe anything of
the Sacrament of the Altar, of Matrimony, of Confession
of Sins, or of any other Sacrament of the Church, or
Article of the Faith, otherwise than it is found discussed
by the Holy Mother the Church; neither turn into doubt
that is defined and decided by the Church, or privily or
openly speak wittingly blasphemous words about the same,
or preach, teach or observe any manner sect or kind of
heresy contrary to the wholesome doctrine of the Church.
   And whosoever shall presume, after publication of
these presents, wittingly and obstinately to attempt the
contrary shall incur in the doing the sentence of excommunication from which he shall, at no time but in the
article of death, be absolved except abjuration of heresy
be first made generally or simply in manner used of the
Church, and he amend himself and for his faults receive
healthy penance at the arbitrament of that Ordinary in
whose territory he is declared and proved to have trespassed.   And if he order himself likewise the second time,
so fall into lapse and thereof be lawfully convicted he
shall be declared by sentence for an heretic in the relapse,
and his goods shall be taken as forfeit and applied to them
that have interest.
   As touching the penance whereof is mention above
made, we will it to be such that if any teach, preach or

hold privily or openly any thing contrary to that which
is determined by the Church in the Decrees, Decretals or
our Constitutions Provincial, or any kind or sect of
heresy, in the Parish Church of that place where he hath
so preached, taught, or holden, upon a Sunday or some
other solemn day or many days at the arbitrament of the
Ordinary of that place, according as he is condemned to
have trespassed little or much, he shall expressly revoke
the self same things which he hath so taught or affirmed.
(This we will to be done in the time of Divine Service
when the great multitude of people is present): and
moreover shall preach, teach and rehearse, effectually and
without fraud and deceit, the things determined by the
Church: and shall furthermore be punished according to
the quality of his demerits as it shall seem to the Ordinary's discretion expedient.

CHAPTER III.

Nullus quoque de articulis.

Canon of Thomas Arundel.

None may presume to dispute openly or privily of the
Articles determined by the Church as they be contained
in the Decrees, Decretals and our Constitutions Pro-
vincialor Synodal, except it be done to have the true
understanding of them, or may call into doubt the
authority of the same Decrees, Decretals or Constitutions
Provincial, or the power of the making of them, and
specially concerning the adoration of the Glorious Cross,
worshipping of Saints images, or pilgrimages making
unto their places, or relics, or against oaths to be made
after the used manner in cases accustomed in both courts,
that is in the spiritual court and temporal, but henceforth
all shall teach commonly and preach that the Cross and
image of the Crucifix and other images of Saints ought
to be worshipped in the memory and honour of them
whom they figure and represent.

And likewise their places and relics with processions,

kneelings, inclinations, censings, kissings, offerings, lights
burning, and pilgrimages, and with all other manners and
fashions as hath been accustomed in our times and our
predecessors, and that oaths made upon the Holy Gospels
of God touched in cases in the law expressed, and in both
courts accustomed may lawfully be given of all that have
interest. And he that affirmeth, preacheth, teacheth or
obstinately meaneth the contrary, except he go from it
under manner and form by us at other times decreed, and
abjure, as it is there provided, he shall incur the pains of
heresy and, in conclusion of relapse and by sentence, shall
be declared for such unto the whole effect of the law.

CHAPTER IV.

Finaliter quia ea quae de novo.

Canon of Thomas Arundel.

Finally for so much as these things which rise newly
and unusedly have need of new and speedy remedy, and
where as greatest jeopardy is there must the wiser provision and the stronger resistance be made, neither yet is
it against justice that the part which is of little value
should be discreetly cut away, that the worthier part may
the perfectlier be nourished, therefore considering (which
things we speak to our heart's sorrow) how the nourish-
ing University of Oxford, which was wont to spread
abroad like as a plenteous vine her fruitful branches to
the honour of God and the manifold profit and defence
of the Church, but now partly joined in to a wild vine
bringeth forth sour grapes, which eaten indiscreetly of
them that repute themselves learned in the laws of God
setteth the children's teeth on edge, and our Province is
infected with divers and unfruitful doctrines and is
spotted with a new damnable name of Lollardy to no little
slander of the same University and great weariness of
them that here be nourished from far and strange parties :
and also to the hurt of the Church of England which was
wont to be defended by the virtuous doctrine of the same

University as with a wall inexpugnable, but now the
stones broken and divided, shall never recover her hurt
again, as it is very likely, except speedy help be provided :
at the supplication therefore of the procurators of the
whole clergy of our Province of Canterbury, and by the
consent and assent of all our fellow brethren and our
suffragans and other prelates being present in this Convocation, of the clergy and the procurators of them that
be absent, we intending wholesomely to provide for the
honour and profit of Holy Mother the Church and of the
said University, lest, when the rivers are purged and
cleansed, the well spring being infected will not suffer the
water to run clear, do statute and ordain that every
warden or provost or custos of a college, or principal of
a hall or Inn of the aforesaid University, diligently
enquire once at the least every month in the college, hall,
or Inn where he ruleth whether any scholar or inhabitant
of such college, hall, or Inn have affirmed, holden, defended, or any wise propounded conclusion, proposition
or opinion sounding evil in the Catholic Faith, or in good
manners contrary to the determination of the Church, but
as the necessary doctrine of his faculty doth require. And
if he find any suspected or defamed therein let him
monish him effectually to cease. And if afterward he
take the same again, or any like contrary to such admonition, besides the pains other times by us appointed he
shall incur in so doing the sentence of the great excommunication. And nevertheless, if he be a scholar that so
taketh them again, what so ever he have done in the same
University from the time of his said admonition, it shall
not stand to him for his form.

And if he be a Doctor, Master, or Bachelor, in so doing
shall be suspended from all scholastical act, and in both
cases they shall lose the right that they had in the college,
hall, or Inn, and shall be really expelled by the same
wardens, custos, provosts, principals, or other to whom it
appertaineth to do it. And without any tarrying, a
Catholic person shall be substituted in his place according
to the lawful manner of that house. And if the wardens,

presidents, or provosts of colleges, or the principals of
halls or Inns, in which such persons suspected, detected,
or defamed do live be negligent about the inquisitions and
executions of the foresaid things by the space of ten days
after they have true knowledge or presumption of the
publication of these presents, in that deed shall incur the
sentence of the great excommunication. And nevertheless in the same deed shall be deprived from all right
which they pretend to have in the colleges, halls, or Inns.
And the same colleges, halls, or Inns shall effectually be
vacant and void. And after lawful declaration made
thereof by them that have interest, new wardens, profestes, presidents, or principals shall be accustomed after
the old manner of the said Universities used when such
colleges, halls or Inns be vacant. But and if the said
wardens, custos, profestes, or principals be defamed
themselves, or be suspected or detected of and upon such
conclusions or propositions, or be defenders, protectors,
or favourers of the same, and be warned by us, or by our
authority, or by the Ordinary of that place, or by his
authority, and yet do not cease then let them be deprived
even by the law from all scholastical privilege of the said
University and from all right and title that they had in
such college, hall, or Inn over and besides other penalties
of which it is before mentioned: and moreover shall
incur the sentence of the great excommunication, but if
any presume wilfully or obstinately, in any case of this
last present constitution or in any other case before
rehearsed, to break these our statutes in any part of them,
although there be another penalty in that same place by
express words limited, yet in the same deed shall he be
made utterly unable and unworthy without any hope of
forgiveness for three years' space to obtain ecclesiastical
benefice within our Province of Canterbury. And shall
nevertheless be canonically punished by the discretion of
his superior according to his merits and the quality of his
excess. Furthermore lest we should seem to wander
uncertainly in manner of process about the premises,
perceiving that though there be a certain likeness and

equalness in divers laws between the crime of heresy and treason, nevertheless the offence is unlike, and it requireth greater punishment to offend the majesty of God than of man. And therefore, seeing it is sufficient to convict him that is accused of treason by certain light tokens and proofs for the jeopardies that may ensue through delays, and seeing that summary and plain process may be made against the party being called in by messenger, by letters, or by proclamation, and so may go forth to the receiving of witnesses and definitive sentence without the said party's answer, we will and ordain and declare *(volumus ordinamus et declaramus)* that, for the easier way of punishing them that fault in the premises, and for the reformation of the Church's division which is thereby greatly hurt, that such as be defamed, denounced, or detected, or be vehemently suspected in any case before specified, or in any other article that soundeth evil in the Catholic Faith, or in good manners, shall be cited by the authority of the Ordinary of that place, or of any other superior, personally if they may so be gotten by letters, or by messenger sworn, or else by proclamation openly made at the place where the transgressor's habitation is, or where he was wont to tarry, or else in his Parish Church if he have a certain dwelling, and in case he have no certain dwelling in the Cathedral Church of that place where he was born and in the Parish Church of that place where they have so preached and taught. And after that lawful certificate be made of the execution of such citation, let process be made against him that is absent and will not appear in pain of such his contumacy, summary and plainly without besynes[a] and figure of judgment, and also without answer making and so forth, to the receiving of witness and other canonical proofs. And after lawful information taken, let the same Ordinary, without any manner delay, give sentence and declare and punish according to the quality of the fault, in manner and form above expressed, and furthermore let him do that justice requireth, the absence of the disobedient notwithstanding.

[a] Strepitu.

TITULUS 6.

Of Apostates.

Praeterea Sunt nonnulli.   Canon of John Peccham.

Furthermore there be some which intendeth, as it appeareth by certain evident facts, to forsake the world for ever, and do shew tokens that they would keep all their life watch in their cloisters in the service of the Lord: and yet notwithstanding, the same being overcome of carnal desire, return to their vomit and go again to the world, worthy to be counted amongst wandering stars: and therefore although the laws do manifestly define that they may not forsake religion utterly, but at the least must continue in some religion[a] that is easier, some nevertheless being without shame, and fearing not the infamy of apostasy after they have plainly declared that they will forsake the world, do leave Jerusalem and return into Egypt, wherefore we ordain *(statuimus)* that the Ordinaries of places shall search with all diligence for such and by subtraction as well of office as of benefice if they have any shall call them back again to the old state, or shall compel them to go to some lesser rule: but, if such apostates be lay persons, let them be compelled by ecclesiastical censure to return to the study of their health: how be it we will not extend this ordinance to them with whom the Apostolic See hath otherwise ordained.

TITULUS 7.

Of them that have slain their children.

Foeminae commoneantur.   Canon of Edmund.

Let women be monished that they nourish their children warely and that they lay not the younglings nigh to them in the night lest they oppress them. Also they may not leave them in their houses where is fire, or nigh hand to the water, alone without a keeper, and let this be shewed them every Sunday.

[a] Religious order.

TITULUS 8.

Of Manslaying.

CHAPTER I.

Si mulier mortua fuerit.   Canon of Edmund.

If a woman be dead in labour and that do plainly appear if the infant be thought to live, let her be cut; so that the woman's mouth be kept open.[26]

CHAPTER II.

Sacri provisione consilii.   Canon of Edmund.

It is enacted *(statutum est)* by provision of the holy Council that if patrons, advocates or feudatories or vice-lords through mischievous boldness presume to slay or maim, by themself or by other, any person of church, vicar, or clerk of the same church, they shall utterly lose patronage, advocation, fee, vicelordship, which they had in the church, and their posterity shall in no wise be received into the college of clerks unto the fourth generation, neither shall obtain the honour of dignity nor prelacy in regular house. And this we will often-times to be denounced in the churches.

TITULUS 9.

Of Theft.

Prohibemus sub interminatione.   Canon of Stephen.

We forbid under the pain of cursing that none retain thieves in service to commit theft, neither suffer them wittingly to dwell in their grounds.

TITULUS 10.

Of a Clerk that is an Hunter.

Statuimus quod siquis clericus.   Canon of Boniface.

We ordain *(statuimus)* that, if any clerk be defamed of trespass committed in forest or park of any man's, and thereof be lawfully convicted before his Ordinary, or do confess it to him, the Diocesan shall make redemption thereof in his goods, if he have goods after the quality of his fault, and such redemption shall be assigned to him to whom the loss, hurt, or injury is done, but if he have no goods let his Bishop grievously punish his person according as the fault requireth, lest through trust to escape punishment they boldly presume to offend.

TITULUS 11.

Of him that hath received Orders by stealth.

Cum secundum Doctores Theologos.

Canon of John Peccham.

Forasmuch as after the mind of doctors of divinity the way of clerks is defensed with seven orders, the sign or mark of every order imprinted in the soul of the receivers, which also by receiving of every order be increased, or augmented with the gifts of grace, except they receive them feignedly, or in deadly sin, it is therefore very expedient that they receive them not thick together, that is to say many at once, for such heaping together doth diminish their reverence and grace and so it followeth that they rebound back from the unworthy through the dishonouring of them: and therefore it is manifestly known that it is against the dignity of the most reverend sacrament to give to any five at once, that is to say four inferior orders with one Holy Order, wherefore in some provinces four smaller orders be not lightly given at once to any person, to the intent that clerks ascending to the service of Christ, singing as it were a song upward, should at length by degrees come to the higher when they were proved in the lower offices: wherefore, inasmuch as we be bound to choose out of every church those things that be godly, that be religious, that be most honest, and bind them together like a fagot in the minds of the English churches, we command (*praecipimus*) that the Bishops in these things follow the ordinances of the Canons : and as concerning the smaller orders, let them be given at the least way some time two and two, for the reverence of the Sacrament when it may with good manner so be done. And they that receive them all at once or singularly, let them be openly instructed in the vulgar tongue of the diversity and distinction of orders, offices and characters, and of the fruit of grace which is contained in every order and is augmented in all that come worthily.

TITULUS 12.

Of the excesses and faults of prelates.

Monemus Rectores Ecclesiarum.   Canon of Edmund.

We admonish *(monemus)* the persons of churches that they labour not to remove their yearly chaplains without a cause reasonable, specially such as be of honest conversation and have laudable witnesses of their honest living, but if there be any slander risen of the incontinence of the parish priest, forsomuch as the person ought to be vigilant herein, therefore, if the Bishop have knowledge thereof, either by common fame or inquisition, before the person denounce it, then shall the person himself be punished at the superior's arbitrament as though he were of Council, and so must we reckon likewise of vicars : and we decree *(decernimus)* as well the persons and vicars to be sharply punished as the parish priests, except they watch and be diligent to denounce the excesses specially of incontinentie, in which the clerks of their parishes be notably found.

TITULUS 13.

Of Privileges.

Sacramentum penitentiae et infra.

Canon of John Peccham.

There be moreover certain which, under pretext of general privileges obtained of the Apostolic See, contrary to the mind of him that gave them such privileges, do despise the Bishop's authority, and, without his pleasure and consent required, thrust in themselves to hear the confessions of their subjects, whose presumptuousness we intending to put down as we be bound to do, forbid *(prohibemus)* under pain of excommunication that none hereafter without the Bishop's licence, either given by express words either probably presumed, hear the confessions of the Bishop's subjects, except by plain tenour of his privilege he be exempt from all jurisdiction ordinary and metropolitan to hear confessions. And if any presume the contrary, process shall be made against them as against rash abusers of their privileges.

TITULUS 14.

Of Canonical Purgation.

CHAPTER I.

Ceterum et infra.   Canon of Stephen.

We thought it straitly to be forbidden *(duximus inhibendum)* that no Archdeacon, or their officials, or other judges compel any to make purgation at the suggestion of their summoners, except the party be otherwise defamed amongst good men and persons of gravity, neither shall presume to be both judges and actors in their own causes, when it is in doubt whether it be due that is exacted and required by them.

CHAPTER II.

Statuimus et infra.   Canon of Boniface.

Moreover if clerks have made their canonical purgation upon such things as was laid and objected against them, and yet nevertheless the lay power taketh their goods or withholdeth them, such takers and withholders shall be compelled unto the restitution of the said goods by censures of the Church.

CHAPTER III.

Clerici pro suis criminibus.   Canon of John Peccham.

Clerks which have been in hold with the lay power for their faults, and at length be restored to the Church for convicted, may not lightly be delivered, neither light purgation for them may be admitted, but, with all solemnity of the law and with such ripe deliberation, that it may not displease the eyes of the King's majesty, or of any other that may be moved with the desire of justice.

CHAPTER IV.

Item licet et infra.   Canon of John Stratford.

We ordain *(statuimus)* that they which hereafter be defamed of crimes, or excesses of crimes, or excesses, and would purge themself thereof shall not be drawn from one deanery into another, or into such places of the country where victuals and other necessaries be not sold, but, in joining purgation to such as be defamed, the Bishops, Archdeacons and other Ordinaries or their officials shall not appoint them above the number of six hands for the crime of fornication or like crime : and for greater crimes as adultery and such above the number of twelve, under pain of suspension from office, which pain we will them that do contrary to incur in so doing.

TITULUS 15.

Of Pains.

CHAPTER I.

Eternae sanctio voluntatis et infra. Canon of Boniface.

Forsomuch as it oftentimes happeneth Archbishops, Bishops and other inferior prelates to be called in to secular judgment by the King's writs letters, there to make answer for such things as be known merely to appertain to their office and the spiritual court, as if perchance they have admitted or not admitted clerks to churches and chapels vacant or not vacant, and have instituted or not instituted rulers in the same, or have excommunicated their subjects, or denounced them excommunicated, have interdicted, have dedicated churches, have given Orders, have had cognition of causes mere spiritual, as of tithes and oblations and of bounds of parishes and other like, which may not in any wise appertain to the secular court, moreover if they have taken examination of the faults and excesses of their subjects as of perjury, promise-breaking, sacrilege, of violating and troubling of the church liberties (specially seeing the violators and disturbers thereof do fall in the deed doing into the sentence of excommunication by the King's charters granted to the Church of England), or if they have taken cognition betwixt their clerks, or betwixt the lay complaining and their clerks defending in personal actions upon contracts or as contracts, upon trespasses or as trespasses, and also if they have not at the King's commandment compelled ecclesiastical persons amerced in the secular court to pay such amercements, or have not paid the same for them, or if they have exercised their canonical and accustomed jurisdiction in churches or chapels annexed to bishoprics or monasteries when they be vacant by death or resignation of their rulers. And if they have done or have not done any such things as appertaineth unto their offices, we decree and ordain by authority of this present Council that Archbishops, Bishops and other prelates shall not appear when they be called for such spiritual causes, for so much as there is no power given to the lay to judge the Lord's anointed, but ought of necessity obey and follow them.

Notwithstanding for the regard of the King's honour let the higher prelates go or write unto the King that they may not obey such the King's commandments without jeopardy of their order and degree. And in case the King's highness make mention in his attachments, prohibitions, monitions, not of tithes but of the right and title of patronage, not of feigned faith or perjury but of

cattle,[a] not of sacrilege or disturbance of the church
liberties but of the transgression of his subjects and
bailees whose correction he affirmeth to appertain to him,
then let the said prelates intimate and shew unto his
dignity that they take not or intend to take cognition of
patronage of cattle, or other things appertaining to his
court, but of tithes, offences, and other mere spiritual
things appertaining to their office and jurisdiction spiritual
and to the health of souls, monishing and beseech-
ing him that he will not let nor withstand them in the
same. And nevertheless let the Bishop himself go unto the
King and again monish him to look unto his soul's health
and utterly to cease from such commandments : and if he
so cease not then at the denunciation of the Bishop, the
Archbishop, calling to him two or three or more other
Bishops, such as shall please him if they be in his province,
or else the Bishop of London being as Dean of the
Bishops, with two Bishops or more joined to him, shall
go to the King and monish him very diligently, requiring
him to cease from such commandments. And if the King
nevertheless proceed, by himself or by other, unto such
attachments and distresses, disputing such exhortations
and admonitions, then the sheriffs and bailees whatsoever
they be that so attach or distrain the said prelates, shall
be kept off by the sentence of excommunication and suspension made in form of law by the Diocesans of the
places : which thing shall likewise be observed, if the
sheriffs or bailees go forwards in such attachments or
distresses in the time that such monitions be made to the
King as beforesaid : and if the sheriffs or bailees continue
in their obstinacy then the places where they dwell and
their lands, which they have in the Province of Canterbury, by authority of this present Council shall be put
under ecclesiastical interdiction by the Diocesans of those
places at the denunciation of the Diocesan within whose
Bishopric such distresses be made. And if they be clerks
that so attach, or be beneficed, they shall be suspended
from office : and if they go forth in their malice, they

[a] i.e. chattels.

shall be compelled to cease and to make satisfaction by subtraction of the provends of their benefices. And such as be not beneficed shall not be admitted by the space of five years if they be presented to any ecclesiastical benefice in our Province of Canterbury : and the clerks that indicted such briefs of attachment or distrains or did write them or seal them or gave help or counsel unto them shall be canonically punished : and whatsoever clerk by any means be suspected in any of the premises, he shall not be admitted to obtain ecclesiastical benefice until he have canonically purged himself thereof. And if the King or other secular power, being competently monished, do not revoke such attachments, the Bishop that is strained shall put under ecclesiastical interdiction the lands, towns, villages and castles which the King or other secular power do obtain in his bishopric. And if the King or other secular power continue in their hardness the other co-bishops, counting such distresses as common unto the injury of them all, and to the common injury of the Church, shall by authority of this present Council put under ecclesiastical interdiction cities, lands, lordships, boroughs, castles and villages as many as be within their bishoprics of the King's or of other secular power.

And if neither so the King revoke such attachment and distrains within twenty days after, or by that means aggravate his hand against the Church, the Archbishop and Bishops shall put their dioceses under ecclesiastical interdiction. The same thing shall be done in the lands, castles, boroughs, having regalities in the said province. And if any bishop be found negligent or slack in this behalf, let him be grievously reproved by his metropolitan, and, if he continue in his negligence, let him be canonically punished by the same. And nevertheless his diocese, by the authority and consent of all the prelates and his authority and consent given in this present Council, shall stand under ecclesiastical interdiction. And in case any bishop or ecclesiastical judge or inferior prelate, being compelled by such distrains, do appear before the King or his justiciaries to allege the privilege of his court,

N

except it be in a case by the law permitted, or of his own free will do appear before them to monish them that they cease from the said injuries, and the acts of his process be then required of him, that by them it may appear whether he have proceeded in any of the said cases or like, contrary to the King's prohibition, or if oaths, excusations, or purgations be required therein, he shall in nowise exhibit his acts or give any oath for so much as such instruments may be exhibited if it be necessary of the parties, or of one of them.

And if he be a clerk that is herefor arrested, the Diocesan of that clerk so arrested or attached, or the Archbishop, or the Bishop of London as the Dean of Bishops, with certain Bishops associate, shall require him, as though he were a Bishop that were arrested, and shall punish the withholders, yea and if it be necessary in this case they shall proceed unto the pains before noted.

CHAPTER II.

Ad haec et infra.   Canon of Boniface.

Inasmuch as it often happeneth that certain clerks do take by the lay power churches parochial or prebendal having cure of souls and be intruded into the same without authority of the Church, we ordain *(statuimus)* a clerk so intruded by himself, or by the lay power, in church or prebend, shall by the due order of the law be excommunicated and for an excommunicated shall be denounced by the Diocesan of that place and shall lack that benefice for ever in so doing. And if he continue with obstinate mind in such intrusion the space of two months after sentence given against him and have other ecclesiastical benefices in other dioceses, at the denunciation of that Bishop in whose diocese he intruded himself or procured himself to be intruded, and whose monition and excommunication he despised by the said time, the profits of those benefices shall be utterly taken from him by the Diocesan of the place until he have satisfied competently.

And if the said intruded stand a year in such sentence

of excommunication he shall not after that be admitted unto ecclesiastical benefice in the Province of Canterbury, but if he be intruded by a procurator being a clerk, like process shall be made against the same procurator, and he shall suffer the same penalties, but if that procurator be a lay person he shall be openly denounced excommunicate. And his master that is absent shall be cited, and if he appear and ratify the deed of any his procurators in that behalf, he shall fall into the said penalties: but if he through contumacy absent himself and be looked for three months' space, being within the realm, shall be wrapped in the sentence of excommunication and shall incur nevertheless the said pains, specially seeing he hath added unto his sacrilege disobedience and contempt. And if he be out of the realm, after the delays for such as be beyond the seas be past, like process shall be made against him being called. And the church or prebend wherein such intrusion is made shall be interdicted. They that are the favourers and workers of such intrusions, if they be clerks, shall incur the said penalties made against clerks, if they be lay they shall be punished with the pains otherwise provided against the lay, the places and lands of such intruders, if they make not amends within a month, shall be under ecclesiastical interdiction, but in case such intrusions be made by the King's power, the King shall be monished to call them back within a competent time, or else the lands and places which the King hath in that diocese where the intrusion is made shall be under interdiction after the manner above noted. And if the intrusion be made by any other nobleman, peer, or of power, he shall be repressed by sentence of interdiction and excommunication as beforesaid: and if he abide such sentence two months, then shall the lands and places which he hath in another diocese be interdicted by the Diocesan of that place: and the said sentence shall not be released until he have made competent satisfaction for the negligence, inobedience and contempt.

CHAPTER III.

Si aliqui clerici.   Canon of Boniface.

If any clerks, having tonsure and clerkship, be taken by the lay power and in the mean time be shaven of malice and hanged or otherwise punished, they that shave them, hang them or otherwise punish them, or give counsel or help thereunto, shall suffer the same penalties : and they that banish such clerks shall likewise be punished.

CHAPTER IV.

Evenit et infra.   Canon of Boniface.

We enact *(statuimus)* that the lay shall be compelled precisely by sentence of excommunication to pay all manner penalties, as well corporal as pecuniary, which they be enjoined by their prelates. And they that will let or stop such penalties to be paid shall be punished by sentence of interdiction and excommunication. And if process be made unto the distraining of places for that cause let process be made against the distrainers by the penalties declared in that behalf.

CHAPTER V.

Item statuimus quod quilibet episcopus.
        Canon of Boniface.

We also enact and ordain *(statuimus)* that every bishop have in his bishopric one or two prisons wherein ungracious clerks, taken in crime or convicted, may be kept according to the commandment of the canons, and if there be any so malicious or incorrigible and so accustomed to mischief that, if he were a layman, he should suffer by the laws of this world, the extremest punishment, such clerk shall be judged to perpetual prison, but in all such faults as be done not of will or purpose but by sudden chance or wrath or perchance madness we will the old laws to be observed.

Chapter VI.

Tantum invaluit. Canon of John Peccham.

The enormity of detestable frailness is so great that some, not regarding the laws nor canons made to stir up the chastity of nuns, fear not to commit sacrilege and sin with them, for the which horrible mischief we, intending to provide remedy, do wrap all committers of such filthiness, as well clerks as lay, in the sentence of the great excommunication, reserving the absolution of such persons only to their bishops, the article of death excepted, in which they may be absolved by any priest, so that if they recover they shall be bound under pain of solemn cursing to confess such their sin to their own Bishop within the space of three months, or else in time of vacation to the keeper of spiritualities, or to the Dean of the Cathedral Church.

Chapter VII.

Quoniam reus et infra. Canon of John Stratford.

We ordain *(statuimus)* that for a fault, notorious, or twice committed, or long continued, no money be received at the second time under pain of restoring the double of such money contrary to this received, which shall be applied within a month after the receiving thereof to the works of the Cathedral Church, and also under the pain of suspension from office, which sentence they that so do receive money shall incur in the doing thereof, except they restore the double within a month. In changing also corporal penance for money, which thing we forbid to be done without a great and urgent cause, the ordinaries of places shall keep such measure that they lay upon the transgressors corporal penance not so excessive heavy, and open that they be compelled by such indirect manner to redeem their penance for some great pecuniary sum, but such commutations, when they shall seem hereafter expedient, shall be made so moderately that neither the receiver be judged a ravener, neither the giver to be ever much loved under the said penalties above rehearsed.

TITULUS 16.

Of Penalties[a] and Remissions.

CHAPTER I.

Quoniam nonnunquam.   Canon of Stephen.

Forsomuch as it happeneth sometimes souls to be in jeopardy through the lack of confessors, forsomuch as the deans rural and persons be ashamed peradventure to confess to their prelates, willing therefore to provide for this sore, we ordain *(statuimus)* that in every deanery through the archdeaconries certain prudent and discreet confessors be appointed by the Bishop of that place to hear the confessions of the deans rural, of persons and priests. In cathedral churches where as be secular canons, let the canons confess to their Bishop or Dean or other persons appointed thereunto by the Bishop or Dean and Chapter.

CHAPTER II.

Cum sacramentum.   Canon of Boniface.

Inasmuch as the sacrament of confession and penance, which is the second table after our shipwreck and the last haven and final refuge of man's failing, is very necessary to every sinner unto health, we straitly command *(praecipimus)* under pain of excommunication that none presume to stop or let, but that such sacrament of penance may be given freely to every one that desireth it, and likewise a space free for confession, which thing is willed principally for them that be in prison, unto whom such sacrament is oftentimes ungentilly (we will not say unfaithfully) denied. And though sometime there be a space given them to confess, yet it is granted so short and so importunate that it putteth the wretched persons rather in jeopardy of discomfort and desperation than in joy and gladness of spiritual comfort.

   [a] Poenitentiis.

CHAPTER III.

In confessione habeat Sacerdos.   Canon of Edmund.

In hearing confession the priest must have a lowly and gentle countenance and his eyes down to the earth, neither may behold the face of the person confessed, specially of a woman, and must patiently hear whatsoever is said, and maintain or support her with the spirit of meekness and softness, and for his power must exhort by all means to make a full confession, otherwise it is no confession, let him enquire used sins, unused he may not but and by circumstances, so that the expert may have a way to confess and the unexpert no occasion to sin : the priest may not enquire the names of the persons with whom the confitent hath sinned, but after confession he may enquire whether he were clerk or lay, monk or priest or dean : and always the greater crimes and specially such as be notorious must be reserved to the higher prelates. These be the greater crimes :—murder, sacrilege, sin against nature or with kin, defiling of virgins or nuns, violent hands on their parents or on clerks, vows broken and such.

There be also causes in which none, but only the Pope or his legate hath power to absolve, notwithstanding the absolution for such may be denied to none in the article of death, but yet it must be conditional that if they recover they shall present themself to the Pope's sight, notwithstanding such shall be sent to the Bishop or his penitentiary. And they that be sent shall always carry with them letters containing the kind of the sin and the chief circumstances, or else let the priest come himself personally, otherwise they shall not be received.

CHAPTER IV.

De poenitentia praecipimus.   Canon of Edmund.

As concerning penance, we command *(praecipimus)* that deacons presume not to give penance but only in these cases when the priest cannot, or is absent, or foolishly or undiscreetly will not, and death is at hand with the sick.

Chapter V.

Cum anima longe pretior.   Canon of Richard.

Seeing the soul is much more precious than the body, under the fear of anatheme, we forbid *(prohibemus)* that no physician ·counsel the sick anything for the bodily health that may turn to the soul's jeopardy or danger : but, when it shall happen him to be called to the sick, before all things let him effectually monish and induce him to call upon the physician of souls, that, after medicine spiritual is provided for the sick, he may the healthsomer proceed in curing the body. They that break this constitution shall not escape the penalty ordained in the Council.

Chapter VI.

Presbyteri stipendiarii et infra.

Canon of Robert Winchelsea.

We ordain *(statuimus)* that no stipendiary priests shall hear the confessions of the parishioners or chaplains in those churches where they have ministered Divine Service, except in cases by the law permitted : if they do the contrary, they shall incur the crime of sacrilege, except they do it by licence asked and obtained of him that is the chief ruler there.

Chapter VII.

Sacerdos in poenitentia injungenda. Canon of Walter.

The priest ought diligently to note and mark the circumstances of the crime, the quality of the person, the kind of the sin, time and place, cause and continuance in the sin, the devout mind of the penitent : and these things considered and diligently weighed and discreetly, let him enjoin the penitent the greater or less penance. Also the priest must choose him a common place to hear confessions, that he may be commonly seen of all the church.

And in privy and hid places the priest shall not receive the confession of any and specially of a woman except it be for the great necessity or infirmity of the penitent. Also no priest may receive another's parishioner unto repentance but by the licence of his priest or bishop. Also the priest must enjoin such penance to the wife that she be not made suspected to her husband of any privy and great crime : the same thing must be observed in the husband. Also for theft, robbery, usury, and covin or fraud, and specially for the withholding of tithes or subtraction of any church right, the priests must diligently beware to enjoin penance but with restitution and satisfaction to be made to them that have suffered the injury or damage, seeing the sin is not forgiven except the thing taken away be restored. Also in crimes very great, cruel and doubtful the priest shall ask counsel of the Bishop or some in his stead, or of some wise and discreet persons by whose counsel he may be certified and know whom and how he may bind and loose. And lest the penitent should fall (which thing God forbid) into desperation the priest must diligently monish him to do whatsoever good thing he can in the mean time, that God may lighten his heart unto penance : and the same thing must he do to him which confesseth his sin and yet will not abstain from it, in which case the gift of absolution cannot be given, seeing it is not read that pardon is given but only to him that amendeth himself. Also the priests must beware that they enquire not the sins or names of the persons with whom the penitent hath sinned, but only the circumstances and quality of the sin, for it is written " God, I have shewed to Thee mine own life and not any other's " : and therefore the confession must be his own that maketh it and not another's confession.

CHAPTER VIII.

Prohibemus quod nullus sacerdos.   Canon of Walter.

We forbid that no priest, fallen into deadly sin, presume to come at the altar to celebrate before he be confessed, neither let him think (as some do that err) believing mortal sins to be put away by general confession.

Also no priest may be so bold through wrath, hatred, nor
fear of death to disclose in any wise the confession of
any by sign, token, beck, or word, generally or specially.
And if he be convicted hereof he ought justly to be dis-
graced without hope of reconciling.

Chapter IX.

Cum saepe contingat.   Canon of Walter.

Seeing oftentimes it happeneth that the rulers of
churches and also some priests and such as be in Holy
Orders, for that (as they think) they be not subjected to
any as concerning the court of penance, either be not confessed at all, either else go to such as have no power to
bind or loose them, we therefore enact *(statuimus)* that
through every Archdeaconry one or two priests apt and
mete, of competent learning and good estimation, be
appointed in every deanery to hear the confession of such
and to enjoin them penance, to whom we will authority
to be given by the Diocesan of that place or one that
keepeth his room, firmly forbidding that no religious
persons or monk or canon anchoret or hermit to be so
bold as to admit the subject of any other unto penance.

Chapter X.

Cum salubiter sit statutum.   Canon of John Peccham.

Forsomuch as it is profitably enacted and ordained that
prelates may not pass in pardons giving the number of
forty days, lest the keys of the Church, by the which the
mystical treasure is committed to be ordered, should be
set at nought, let therefore other, whatsoever they be, take
heed that they, through their manifold indulgencies which
they have obtained of the prelates, bring no rebuke to the
same prelates of the Church by pouring forth in their
preachings indulgencies above the said days, lest they
which ought to be subjected unto the keys cause them to
be light regarded.

CHAPTER XI.

Sacramentum poenitentiae. Canon of John Peccham.

The sacrament of penance, which is the singular remedy for all that suffer shipwreck, through the foolishness of certain priests, doth lack the due fruit and effect. And they which be thought to be lifted above the waves and floods be with more jeopardy thrust down into the deep sea of damnation, while they absolve many in deed whom of right they might not, causing as the prophet saith, for a little corn and a piece of bread the souls to live which in very deed liveth not, as these that absolve in fact such as be excommunicated of the law and specially by the Council of Oxford, for the hurting or troubling of the church liberty or for like mischief condemned in the same Council unto like penalties, or absolve in fact such as be excommunicated for withholding tithes or other church rights : which priests, forsomuch as they be the deceivers of fools and the flatterers of men in their mischievous deeds, putting cushions under the elbows of lewd fellows, it is therefore our part to withstand them. And therefore we straitly command all confessors of our Province of Canterbury that be under us and our fellow Bishops, that hereafter they put not forth their hands to deceive such by the sign and token of absolution, which we know to be of none effect without due satisfaction and special commission of the Archbishop or Bishop, seeing they be froward and continue in their wickedness, for we judge such confessors, or rather such diggers of the devil's dens to sin (and that very grievously, for it cannot be denied but that they consent at the least way privily to the same mischief and do comfort the wicked persons in their ungraciousness) : wherefore let them take heed that they be not wrapt with such in the bond of excommunication : moreover whereas we, of late minding to put down the plurality of benefices by sacrilege usurped, did forbid under pain of excommunication that none in fact should extend their hands to absolve such as were obstinate in their theft and sacrilege, notwithstanding certain priests of Baal, rather than of the Lord which is the Saviour, slaying the souls bought with the blood of Christ and overthrowing the Church doctrine : therefore we, counting verily these as wolves going about to cast down the Lord's vineyards, do again command under the old penalty that they abstain hereafter from absolving such and that they diligently induce the same to renounce the benefices which they have gotten or keep unlawfully : and if they do not, know they themselves to be surely stricken with the lightning of the divine malediction.

Chapter XII.

Praeterea cum juxta.   Canon of John Peccham.

Furthermore although, after the mind of the canons, grievous sins, as incest and the like, which (as most commonly used) through their slander do move an whole city, ought to be corrected with solemn penance, nevertheless, through the negligence dealing of some persons, such penance seemeth as it were forgotten, and consequently boldness to commit such horrible and mischievous deeds to be increased, wherefore we command *(praecipimus)* that such solemn penance henceforth be enjoined according to the canonical ordinance : we also reserve the absolution from wilful murder, whether it be open or privy to the Bishops only except the article of necessity, whereby we intend to refrain the audacity of the inferior confessors and in no case to derogate the reverence of the higher.

Chapter XIII.

Licet a sanctis Patribus.   Canon of John Peccham.

Although it was of late ordained by holy fathers that in every deanery one person or vicar, of sufficient literature and with grace lightened and of fame laudable, should be assigned to hear the confessions of persons, vicars and other priests and ministers of the Church and to enjoin them penance to the intent that there might be the sea of cast work in the entering of the temple according to the sacraments of the figurative temple, nevertheless it hath not hitherto been used in the manners of the clergy, not without the manifold injuries of God in the ministration of sacraments and celebrating of masses, which rather should be called execrations and cursings, wherefore we renewing the said ordinance from disuse command *(praecipimus)* the same from henceforth inviolably to be observed and kept, notwithstanding we intend not by this but the said priests may go to other common penitentiaries if they will, so that they do it for the sacrament of penance.

Chapter XIV.

Confessiones mulierum.   Canon of Simon Sudbury.

The confessions of women must be heard without the veil in open place as appertaining to the eyes but not to the ear : let the lay also be admonished to make their confession even in the beginning of Lent : and in all times shortly upon their fall, lest one sin through his weight and heaviness draw and hale them unto another. Moreover let no priest presume to enjoin them that be confessed to cause masses to be sung or said in part or full penance notwithstanding he may counsel them thereunto.

Chapter XV.

In confessionibus et praedicationibus.
                                Canon of Simon Sudbury.

Let this thing be oftentimes shewed, and as it were trodden in to the hearts of the lay people, both in confessions and preachings and specially in great solemnities, that all commixtion and meddling of male and female, only it be excused by matrimony, is deadly and mortal sin. And if the priest shall be found negligent in denouncing and declaring of this wholesome doctrine let him be canonically punished as a fornicator or consenter unto fornication in so doing.

CHAPTER XVI.

Confessiones ter in annis.   Canon of Simon Sudbury.

Three times in the year let confessions be made, and so often let the lay be admonished to take their rights, at Easter, at Whitsuntide and at Christmas : howbeit first they ought to prepare and make themselves ready by some abstinence which they must keep by the priest's counsel. And whatsoever he be that shall not at the least once in the year be confessed unto his own priest, and at Easter at the least receive the Sacrament of Thanksgiving, except by the priest's counsel he think it better to abstain and forbear, both while he is living let him be driven from church entering, and when he is dead let him lack Christian burial. And let this be oftentimes published in the churches.

TITULUS 17.

Of the Sentence of Excommunication.

CHAPTER I.

Auctoritate Dei Patris.   Canon of Stephen.

By the authority of God the Father Almighty and of the Blessed Virgin Mary and of all Saints, and by authority of this present Council, we excommunicate all such as presume maliciously to rob or defraud churches, that is to say ecclesiastical persons of their rights and titles, or through malice labour and go about to break or trouble their liberties : we also wrap in the sentence of excommunication all them that presume injuriously to trouble and disquiet the peace and tranquillity of our lord the King and of his realm, and that labour and contend to withhold unjustly our lord the King's rights.

We also add unto these, declaring all them to be knit in like sentence, whatsoever they be, that wittingly bear false witness and procure false witness to be bourne, and also that wittingly bring forth such witnesses or suborn and instruct such in cause of matrimony, as when plea is made against matrimony, or else to the disinheriting of any person. Also we excommunicate all them which for cause of lucre, hatred, or favour, or for any other cause put upon any man maliciously any manner crime, by means whereof he is defamed with good men and sad, so that at the least he is put to his purgation or is otherwise grieved. All manner advocates also we excommunicate which in cause of matrimony put forth maliciously exceptions, or cause them to be put forth to the intent that true matrimony should not come to true effect and end, or that contrary unto justice the process of the cause should be kept back and hang the longer in judgment.

Furthermore we knit up all them in the sentence of excommunication which in the vacation of any church move or put forth maliciously the question or doubt of patronage, or in any wise procure the same to put forth or moved, that so they might defraud the true patron of the collation and gift of that church at the least wise for that time.

We also excommunicate all them which for love of lucre, hate, or favour, or otherwise, condemn and despise to execute our lord the King's commandment given out against persons excommunicated which despise the keys of the Church.

Chapter II.

Ut Archidiaconi et infra.   Canon of Stephen.

We ordain *(decernimus)* moreover the profit with the honour of the spiritual orders well considered that no archdeacon or other officials shall be so bold as to promulgate and publish the sentences of excommunications, suspensions or interdictions against any persons where the crime is not manifest, unless he do canonically admonish him before : if any, contrary to the premises, do excommunicate any man, he shall run into the danger prescribed against such offenders by the Convocation and Council holden at Lateran, that is to say for such suspension or interdiction he shall be punished by the arbitrament of his superiors and this also must be observed of the higher prelates.

CHAPTER III.

Praeterea contingit.   Canon of Boniface.

Furthermore it happeneth sometime that some excommunicated persons which by the commandment of their prelates (according to the custom of the realm) be taken and committed to prison, sometime by the King's power, sometime by the sheriff or other bailiffs without the consent of the prelates at whose commandment the delivery of such captives ought to be made, are without any manner of satisfaction at all delivered and set at liberty, and oftentimes such excommunicated persons be not taken neither by the King's letters for their attachment granted, and also sometimes the said King, sheriffs and bailiffs do communicate and company with the said excommunicate and openly denounced persons, despising the keys of the Church, and all to the subversion of the liberties of the Church and the peril of their souls. For this cause we, willingly to provide a convenient remedy against these diseases, do ordain *(statuimus)* and make that all excommunicate persons that be so taken, and as aforesaid delivered out of prison, shall be, to the great detestation both of them that be delivered and also of the deliverers, openly and solemnly with bell, book and candle be excommunicated, and for excommunicated and accursed persons be declared and denounced in such places as the Ordinaries shall think expedient. And the sheriffs and other bailiffs which did deliver them and make no manner of satisfaction and amends to the Church for the same shall be accursed after the due order of the law, and when they be accursed shall solemnly be denounced and declared: howbeit if they do the said act by the King's commandment they may be the more easily and gently handled at the arbitrament of the Ordinaries. But if it fortune the accustomable writ *de excommunicato capiendo* to be denied, at such time as it chanceth to be required, in especial where it ought to be awarded by the laudable custom of the realm, the same lord and King must be warned by the prelate which signifieth and presenteth the person that should be taken, and for the same writeth unto the King that it might please him to grant the said writ and cause the same to pass, which if he will not do all the cities, castles, boroughs and villages which the said King hath in his diocese that so doth write shall be by the Bishop so writing interdicted, until such time as the said writ *de excommunicato capiendo* and due execution of the same be awarded : and against such as do communicate with excommunicate persons let process be made after the censures and laws of the Church.

Chapter IV.

Item contra gravamina et infra.   Canon of Boniface.

We ordain *(statuimus)* that somners, apparitors or bedells or Archdeacons or deans shall not themselves give or make sentences of excommunications, suspensions, interdictions, neither shall denounce nor declare the same given or made by other without they have special letters of their masters for the same. And if it be otherwise presumed the sentences so given or made shall be of none effect by the law, neither shall be regarded, seeing in very truth they can bind no man thereby : and the bedells which offend the said statute, and be proved onerous or injurious to the subjects of their masters, shall have grievous punishment and be bound to restore to the suppliants so vexed double value for their damages.

Chapter V.

Cum saepius Domino Regi.   Canon of Boniface.

Forasmuch as it hath been oftentimes by false suggestions shewed the King and his Justices that the prelates and spiritual judges take cognition and knowledge of the title and right of patronage, of cattle and of other things appertaining to the King's court and judgment to the prejudice of the said King and his laws, when the same prelates and judges, according to their duty done, exercise their office upon tithes and the offences and trespasses

o

of the subjects of their jurisdiction, let such delators and
cursed suggesters be warned that they cease and rest from
such suggestion and tale bearing; for, if it fortune the
prelates and spiritual judges in such wise blasphemed to
be damaged and hurted by the secular power through such
delation and tale bearing, they shall be openly accursed as
strivers against the Church liberties, until such time as
they have competently recompensed and satisfied the
judges and also the parties for their expenses, damages
and injuries which they have borne by means of such
suggestion.

Chapter VI.

Cum malum et infra.   Canon of John Peccham.

We give commandment *(praecipimus)* unto every of
the priests of this Province that on every Sunday immediately following the celebration and keeping of rural
chapters they expound openly to such as they have cure
of the sentences of excommunication following :—First
of all, verily they be accursed by authority of a Council
kept of Oxford by Stephen the Archbishop of Canterbury
a man of holy memory, which doth maliciously presume
to deprive or take from churches the right or, through
malice or contrary unto justice, do contend to break or disturb the liberties of the same, whereby we perceive all
them to be tied in the danger and in the bond of excommunication, whosoever obtaineth letters from any lay
court to let or hinder the process of spiritual judges in all
such causes as by the veredicte of holy canons be known
to appertain to the judgment of the spiritual court.

Secondly all such that do trouble or presume to trouble
without a reasonable cause the peace and tranquillity of
our sovereign lord the King of the realm, and also such
as go about and labour unjustly to withhold the King's
rights whereof, we perceive not only such to be excommunicated as do suscitate error of war or contention, but
also all open and common thieves, and also all spoilers
and pirates with all such as do temerariously impugn the
justice of the realm.

Thirdly are excommunicated all they which wittingly bear false witness, or do procure any man to bear, or which knowingly bring forth such witnesses to let just matrimony, or to procure thereby the disinheriting of another person.

Fourthly all advocates be excommunicated which maliciously by any manner of exceptions do hinder true matrimony whereby it doth not come to good effect, or for any manner of causes by any means do cause contrary to justice the processes of the Church longer to hang undecided.

Fifthly be excommunicated all such which for gains, hatred, or favour do lay a default to any person maliciously, whereby he is defamed with good and discreet men of sadness, so that he is driven to his purgation or is otherwise grieved.

Sixthly all they be excommunicated which maliciously move or procure any doubtful question to be moved concerning the right of patronage in the vacation of any church, that by such means they may hinder the very and true patron from the gift of the said church at the least wise for that time.

Also seventhly all such be excommunicated as rancorously doth despise to execute the King's commandment *de excommunicatis capiendis,* or be in cause and let that such excommunicates be not taken or procureth the unrightful deliverance of the same against the ordinance of the Church.

Also eighthly all they be accursed in the Council of Octobone of good memory, the legate, which do receive anything or take any bribe or gift for to hinder the peace either for the agreement of such as be at variance in the law, until such time they do restore to the giver whatsoever is received : they also be excommunicate by the same Octobone which take away, or waste or wrongfully layeth hand upon any part of the houses, manors or granges or any places of Archbishops or of any other spiritual persons contrary to the will of the said lords, or against the will and mind of the keepers of the said goods,

by the which sentence they be bound and can not be
absolved until they have competently satisfied such wrong.
Also by the said Council all such be accursed that do
draw away violently offenders fleeing to the church or
churchyard or cloister, or stop from such persons their
necessary food which otherwise would be brought to
them, or by violence carrieth away from such places any
other man's goods left in the same place, or causeth such
goods to be carried, or ratifieth and upholdeth such con-
veying and carriage made and done in his name by his
familiars or servants, or openly or secretly do assent or
give counsel thereto.   Also all such be excommunicate by
all Archbishops and Bishops of England which cometh
or doeth against any thing contained in the Great Charter
of the King which sentence is often conformed and approved by the authority of the Apostolic See.

CHAPTER VII.

Superno Dei Munere.   Canon of John Stratford.

Edward the excellent and famous king of England,
receiving from above through heavenly gift of God fervent mind and desire to have the peace of the Church and
Realm of England firmly observed, desiring by his letters
long time passed us and other co-bishops of the said realm
that common malefactors and troublers of holy Church's
peace and his, as felons and also maintainers of felons,
conspirators, false swearers in assizes and juries and all
such that knowing doth forswear themselves before the
King's justices, the bearers of false complaints, maintainers and favourers of the same, by whom the troubling of
the peace and the violating and breaking of the liberty and
right of the Church and of the realm within the same
realm is plainly known to be procured, might in every
diocese be bridled and kept down by ecclesiastical punishment, willing to have them for their grievous excesses in
these enormities to be bound and wrapped in the sentence
of the more grievous excommunication or else openly to
be pronounced accursed, whereupon we of a meek mind,

greatly provoked by the laudable enticement of the said King, desirous to extermine the bold arrogance of such miscreants, will and pronounce all malefactors before named which do wittingly hereafter offend, in our Province of Canterbury by the authority of this present Council in so doing, to run in danger of the sentence of the grievouser excommunication, whose absolution we will be reserved to ordinaries of the places where the trespass is done or else (if their places be void or vacant which shall exercise there the Bishop's jurisdiction) of the cathedral churches of the sees, unless it be in the article of death, but yet that the mischievous deeds of such transgressors may so much the better be eschewed, the more solemnly and openly the same offenders be denounced excommunicated, this Provincial Council approving the same, we give commandment that all and every such malefactor before named in every cathedral church, college and parish church of our before named Province of Canterbury the first Sunday of Lent, and in the Feast of Corpus Christi and two other solemn feasts yearly, be openly denounced accursed in genere with the rehearsal of reservation of the aforesaid absolution.

Chapter VIII.

Praecipimus quod Sententiae.

Canon of John Peccham.

We give in commandment *(praecipimus)* that the sentences of the more excommunication be published in churches four times in the year, that is to wit, the first Sunday after the Feast of Saint Michael and the Sunday in the middes of Lent, in the Feast of the Trinity and in the Sunday next after the Feast of Saint Peter called *ad vincula,* the candles lighted and the bells rung, with the Cross and other solemnities as it is convenient.

TITULUS 18.

On the signification of words.

Quanquam ex-solventibus et infra.

Canon of John Stratford.

We declare *(declaramus)* by the provision of this Council *sylvam sceduam* that is to say copse wood to be such which, of what so ever kind of trees it be, is for a special purpose kept and nourished to be cut down and which also so cut down afterward spring again of the same stumps or roots, and of it so increased the tithes, that is to wit real and predeal, to be paid to the baptizing or mother churches. Also the possessors of such woods to be compelled by the Canon Law to give tithes of those trees cut down in the same woods likewise, as of hay and of all manner of corn, and that by the censure of the Church.

HERE ENDEN THE CONSTITUCYONS PROVINCYALL.

NOTES TO BOOK I.

1. Page 6. A mortuary was a fee as defined in the Canon. By legislation under Henry VIII. it was retained only in the cases where the estate of the deceased was of more than £10 value. In other cases it was to be compounded by a burial fee of one shilling. In the course of time, mortuaries tended to disappear and the shilling fee only remained. But in some cases the surviving mortuary fees were compounded for in the Tithe awards of 1836 onwards.

2. Page 7. The sale of tithes is here regulated by custom. Tithes themselves are dealt with in Book III., Titulus 16, where they are regarded as a species of oblation. This is interesting because in both places the " title " is controlled by custom and not by legislation or documents. It makes it doubtful whether in the fifteenth century the title of the Ethelwulf donations would have been accepted as the basis of the ownership of tithe.

3. Page 10. In a gloss here Lyndwood quotes S. Thomas Aquinas to the effect that fasting is not of the substance of the Sacrament of Confirmation but of its well-being.

Hoc tamen non est de substantia sacramenti sed de bene esse.

4. Page 11. Bishop-bonds. The original is fascias sive ligaturas deferant competentes. *Fasciæ* was the name of bandages used for wounds. *Ligaturæ* was a more general term. Their use was to prevent the oil used being accidentally removed from the confirmee's forehead.

5. Page 11. Anoiling=extreme unction.
6. Page 17. " So to sing," original celebrare.
7. Page 24. Thobie=Tobias.
8. Page 24. Craking—pronounced cracking. Still in use in Yorkshire=boasting. Here boasting is the translation of ostentatio.
9. Page 27. The mark was 13/4.
10. Page 28. Presidents of Churches or Chapels were those who were neither Rectors nor Vicars, such as Decani, Præpositi, Magistri, Custodes, Guardiani, Plebani, Archipresbyteri—et alii consimiles.
11. Page 30. Procurator is Proctor writ long.

NOTES TO BOOK II.

12. Page 34. The normal arrangement is exemplified by the presidence of the unbaptised Constantine presiding at the Council of Nicæa. The arrangement safeguards the interests of the State.
13. Page 42. (A.) Cum regimine chori. The Precentor appointed four canons for double feasts and two for simple feasts to lead the chant. The appointed Canons were called Rectores chori. They were appointed either by rota or at the discretion of the Precentor and were selected from the upper or second bench according to the dignity of the feast. Feasts so observed were described as cum regimine chori (Procter on Prayer Book). Feasts not so observed were described as sine regimine chori. See Vol. II. Henry Bradshaw Society's *Directorium Sacerdotum*.

(B.) Sarum use. This was a peculiarity of the English Church.
Elsewhere the Metropolitical Church set the standard.
14. Page 46. *Statute.* Lyndwood's gloss is Potest enim episcopus
sua Diocesi Statutum facere, quo ligari debeant sui subditi; et tale
statutum dicitur canon episcopalis. Nota tamen, quod contra canones
non potest episcopus aliquid statuere.
It is assumed that the bishop will act constitutionally so far as his
synod is concerned.

NOTES TO BOOK III.

15. Page 55. Raschenes=rashness, "ex temeritate."
16. Page 60. Corrodies. Pensions to relations of founders of
religious houses.
17. Page 62. Gage, pignus, property held as security.
18. Page 65. Insinuation of testaments. Publication of wills. By
English custom this was the duty of Ecclesiastical judges.
19. Page 74. Prædial tithe. Sic dictam quia ratione prædiorum
debetur. Selden, on Tithes, page 207, of 1618 edition, describes these
tithes as "of mixed profits."
20. Page 89. Not to pass the number of waiters=not to exceed
the number of retinue (numerum evectionis) assigned—5 or 6.
21. Page 92. Customary proxies. In England, custom had arranged
that the Archdeacon received in money 7/6, that is, 1/6 for himself
and his horse, and 1/- for each attendant.
22. Page 106. This was one of the minor differences between
English and foreign custom.
23. Page 106. Reddites=reditus=Income.
24. Page 107. Church's Liberties=Rights of Sanctuary. "Ad
immunitatem Ecclesiæ fugientes." Immunitas est Privilegium quo
gaudet Ecclesia ut in ambitu suo non fiat pugna.

NOTE TO BOOK IV.

25. Page 116. There is little said here directly about Matrimony.
The inference is that Marriage customs were very well known and
observed in England and that there was no remarkable difference
between those customs and the Church Law as set out in general
canons and general practice.

NOTE TO BOOK V.

26. Page 134. Possibly a provision against suffocation. Possibly,
also, there was a mystical interpretation.

PRINTED IN GREAT BRITAIN BY
THE FAITH PRESS, LTD., LEIGHTON BUZZARD.

9 781409 723905